# Contents

# The 5 C's that lives in each other

Christ  -  Commitment  - Communication
Compromise  -  Change

## Dedication

This book is dedicated to the countless families who strive daily to build strong relationships rooted in faith. It is a testament to their unwavering commitment, their enduring love, and their courageous pursuit of a Christ-centered life. To those who have faced trials and emerged stronger, to those who persevere through challenges with unwavering hope, and to those who find joy and peace amidst life's storms – this book is a heartfelt tribute to your resilience and faith.

It is my prayer that these pages offer encouragement, guidance, and a renewed sense of purpose as you continue your journey of building a fulfilling family life grounded in the unwavering love and grace of our Lord Jesus Christ. May the wisdom shared within these pages be a beacon of light, guiding your steps and strengthening the bonds of love that unite you. To those who seek a deeper understanding of God's plan for family life, may this book illuminate the path towards a more meaningful, joyful, and spiritually enriching journey together. This work is a celebration of the beautiful, complex, and often challenging tapestry of family life, weaving together biblical truths with relatable stories, offering comfort, hope, and practical guidance to navigate life's many twists and turns. May God continue to bless and guide you always.

## Preface

For many years, I've had the privilege of walking alongside families, witnessing their joys and sorrows, their triumphs and struggles. In countless counseling sessions, I've observed a recurring theme: the deep longing for true fulfillment, for strong relationships, and for a sense of peace that transcends the challenges of daily life. This book is born from those experiences, from the heartfelt conversations and shared moments that have shaped my understanding of the profound connection between faith, family, and lasting happiness. It is a culmination of years spent studying scripture, reflecting on personal experiences, and observing the transformative power of God's love in countless lives.

I believe that true fulfillment isn't found in relentless striving or the pursuit of worldly achievements, but in a deep, abiding faith in God and a wholehearted commitment to His plan for our lives. The principles outlined in this book, rooted in the teachings of **Matthew, Luke, and Psalms** , offer a practical guide for navigating the complexities of family life while prioritizing spiritual growth and meaningful connections. This book isn't intended as a rigid set of rules, but rather a compassionate invitation to explore the transformative power of God's grace and the enduring strength that comes from embracing His love. My prayer is that it will serve as a catalyst for reflection, a source of hope, and a guide towards creating families built on a solid foundation of faith, love, and unwavering commitment. May it inspire you to deepen your relationship with God and cultivate stronger, more meaningful connections with those you love most. May the wisdom found within these pages empower you to embrace the beautiful journey of family life, fully trusting in God's unwavering love and guidance along the way.

## Introduction

In today's fast-paced world, it's easy to get caught up in the whirlwind of daily life, striving for achievements and success while neglecting the most precious relationships in our lives – those within our families. This book explores the biblical foundation for building strong, joyful, and fulfilling family relationships. We will examine the core principles essential for creating a thriving family environment, grounded in a deep commitment to God. Through insightful scriptural references from **Matthew, Luke,** and **Psalms,** we will unravel the secrets to cultivating a Christ-centered home, where faith is not merely a Sunday ritual but a vibrant, everyday reality.

We'll delve into the practical application of biblical principles, offering tools and strategies for improving communication, strengthening commitment, navigating conflicts through compromise, and adapting to change with grace and faith. The journey towards true fulfillment is not always easy. It requires a willingness to surrender our own will, to trust in God's plan, and to embrace the transformative power of His love. This book is an invitation to embark on that journey together, exploring the five essential "C's" of strong relationships: Christ, Communication, Commitment, Compromise, and Change. Each "C" will be explored in depth, illustrating how they intertwine to create a strong foundation for lasting and fulfilling relationships.

We will examine real-life situations, both from the Bible and contemporary experience, to showcase how these principles play out in the everyday dynamics of family life. Personal anecdotes and practical advice are intertwined with biblical wisdom, offering a unique blend of spiritual insight and relatable guidance. This book is not just about theoretical concepts; it's about practical application, empowering you to build a family life characterized by love, joy, peace, and unwavering faith in God's plan. Prepare to be challenged, encouraged, and inspired as we explore the path toward building strong, fulfilling families that reflect God's glory.

## Chapter 1: The Foundation of Fulfillment: Christ at the Center

-Christ as the Cornerstone of Strong Relationships

-Cultivating a Christ-Centered Home Environment

-Overcoming Obstacles Through Faith

-The Power of Prayer in Family Life

-Finding Rest in Gods Sovereignty

-Christ as the Cornerstone of Strong Relationships

## Christ as the Cornerstone of Strong Relationships

The cornerstone of any truly strong and enduring relationship, whether it be marital, familial, or even within a close-knit community of friends, is a shared foundation. And what better foundation can there be than the unwavering love and guidance of Christ? It's not merely about attending church services together or engaging in rote religious practices; it's about weaving the very fabric of faith into the everyday fabric of family life. This involves embracing Christ not just as a figurehead, but as the living, breathing center of your shared existence.

Consider the family of Abraham. While his journey was far from perfect, marked by moments of doubt and wavering faith, it was his unwavering commitment to God, his trust in the divine plan, that ultimately defined his legacy. The strength of his family, his descendants, became a testament to the power of a God-centered life, passed down through generations.

Abraham's willingness to obey God's command, even when it seemed illogical or challenging, laid the groundwork for a legacy of faith that shaped the history of Israel. This wasn't merely obedience for obedience sake; it was an expression of deep trust and love for God, a trust that became the foundation of his family unit and its enduring strength. His unwavering faith in the face of adversity and his steadfast reliance on God shaped not only his life but the lives of his descendants for centuries to come.

The same principle applies to the modern family. A shared faith isn't a magic bullet that eliminates all conflict; rather, it acts as a powerful adhesive, holding the family together amidst the inevitable storms of life. When trials and tribulations strike —job loss, illness, grief, or the everyday stresses of modern living—a shared faith provides an anchor, a source of strength and comfort in the midst of adversity. It's within the shared experience of prayer, of seeking solace and guidance together in scripture, that families find the resilience to navigate challenges, emerging stronger on the other side. The challenges of life often test the strength of any relationship; however, a foundation in Christ provides a resilience and stability that can endure even the most difficult of storms.

This doesn't negate the importance of open communication, commitment, compromise, and the ability to adapt to change—the other crucial elements of a thriving family. Instead, faith in Christ underpins and strengthens these essential components. Open communication becomes easier when you share a common belief system, a shared language of faith to draw upon in times of conflict. Commitment takes on a deeper meaning when viewed through the lens of God's covenant love, a love that endures beyond earthly trials and tribulations. Compromise becomes less about personal sacrifice and more about mutual respect, guided by the example of Christ's selfless love. And the inevitable changes in life are met not with fear and uncertainty, but with a trust in God's sovereign plan, knowing that He is working all things for the good of those who love Him.

Think of the families depicted in the Gospels. The family of Nazareth, though certainly not without its challenges, provides a powerful example. While the scriptures don't detail every nuance of their family life, we see a family bound together by faith, facing immense challenges with courage and unwavering trust in God. Jesus's ministry, His very life, was an embodiment of his familial and communal values. He didn't shy away from difficult conversations, but instead engaged in them with empathy and grace, modeling the importance of open communication and forgiveness.

His own unwavering commitment to his Father's will provides a potent example for families seeking to strengthen their bonds through a shared faith. The family of Nazareth, with all its trials, became a beacon of faith, demonstrating the transformative power of living a life devoted to Christ.

The **book of Proverbs** also offers numerous insights into the importance of building a Godly family. Proverbs emphasizes the importance of wisdom, understanding, and righteous conduct within the family unit. The importance of a godly mother and father is highlighted, setting an example of faith and devotion for their children. The book also touches upon the challenges of raising children, reminding parents of the importance of discipline, guidance, and unwavering support. This family model, rooted in faith and wisdom, illustrates the impact of a Christ-centered home on shaping future generations. Proverbs encourages a holistic approach to family life, encompassing spiritual, moral, and relational aspects, creating a blueprint for a strong and loving family.

We see this reflected in countless families throughout history. Families who have faced unimaginable hardships – persecution, poverty, war – have found strength and solace in their shared faith. I've witnessed this firsthand in my pastoral work. I've counseled families struggling with illness, job loss, and even the death of loved ones, who have found an incredible resilience and even a profound sense of peace in their shared faith. Their ability to draw upon their spiritual resources together, to find comfort in prayer and in the scriptures, has been remarkable. These families often described a renewed sense of intimacy and mutual support, a deepening of their bond through shared adversity. Their faith, shared and actively lived, was the glue that held them together and guided them through the darkest of times. Their resilience underscores the profound impact of a shared faith on family strength.

The power of shared prayer, in particular, cannot be overstated. Family prayer isn't merely about reciting words; it's about creating a space of vulnerability, honesty, and mutual support. It's about acknowledging your reliance on God together, sharing your joys and sorrows, your hopes and fears, before a loving and compassionate Father. This shared vulnerability, this willingness to lay bare your hearts before God and before each other, fosters a powerful sense of intimacy and unity. The consistent practice of shared prayer acts as a spiritual lifeline, renewing strength and fostering mutual understanding. It's in these moments of shared vulnerability that families often find the deepest connection and build a stronger and more resilient foundation.

Building a Christ-centered home isn't about rigid adherence to a set of rules; it's about intentionally creating a space where faith is lived, breathed, and celebrated. This means incorporating prayer into your daily routines, engaging in family Bible study, and participating in acts of service together. It means modeling a life of faith, demonstrating integrity, compassion, and forgiveness in your interactions with each other and the world around you. It's about living your faith visibly and authentically, letting your actions speak louder than words. The goal is not to create a perfect family, but a family that is constantly striving toward holiness, constantly growing in their faith and in their love for one another. The journey is far from perfect, but the destination, a family firmly rooted in the love of Christ, is a goal worth pursuing with all our hearts.

The impact extends beyond the immediate family unit. Families grounded in faith often become anchors in their communities, extending their love and support to others. Their shared faith motivates them to engage in service, to reach out to those in need, and to contribute to the well-being of their community. This outward focus serves as a testament to their inner strength, demonstrating that a strong faith not only strengthens families but also enriches their communities. This outward expression of their faith serves as a testimony to the transformative power of their commitment.

In conclusion, Christ is not merely a figurehead to be placed at the center of a family; He is the very cornerstone upon which strong, lasting, and fulfilling relationships are built. It's through a shared faith, a commitment to living a life guided by His teachings, that families find the resilience to overcome challenges, the intimacy to navigate conflicts, and the strength to build a legacy of love, hope, and unwavering faith. This is not merely an abstract ideal but a reality achievable through intentional effort and unwavering commitment to the God who is the source of all love and strength. The journey may have its obstacles, but with Christ at the center, the destination—a life of fulfillment and enduring love—is a promise worth pursuing.

## Cultivating a Christ-Centered Home Environment

Building a Christ-centered home isn't about imposing rigid rules or creating a sterile, overly pious atmosphere. It's about cultivating a loving, vibrant environment where faith permeates every aspect of family life, from the mundane to the momentous. It's about creating a space where God's presence is felt, not just on Sundays, but every single day. Think of it less as a structured program and more as a gentle, consistent weaving of faith into the very fabric of your family's existence.

One of the most powerful ways to achieve this is through consistent, shared prayer. This doesn't require lengthy, eloquent pronouncements. Simple, heartfelt prayers, offered together as a family, can profoundly impact the atmosphere of your home. Begin and end your days with prayer, thanking God for His blessings and seeking His guidance throughout the day. Incorporate prayers before meals, transforming what might otherwise be a routine into an opportunity for gratitude and connection with God. Even during times of difficulty or conflict, turning to prayer as a family can create a powerful sense of unity and reliance on a higher power. Remember, prayer isn't just about asking; it's also about listening, allowing for a space of quiet reflection and a chance to hear God's voice together. Consider designating a specific time each day for family prayer – perhaps during breakfast or before bedtime.

Beyond prayer, regular Bible study forms another essential pillar. It doesn't have to be a formal, academic exercise. Choose age-appropriate passages and make it interactive. For younger children, picture books that tell biblical stories can be engaging and memorable. For older children and teens, discussion-based studies can stimulate critical thinking and foster a deeper understanding of God's word. With adults, delve into more complex passages and explore their relevance to daily life.

Don't be afraid to engage in open, honest discussions about what you are reading, sharing your thoughts and interpretations. The goal is not just to learn the Bible but to allow it to shape your thinking, attitudes, and actions.

The integration of faith into daily life extends beyond prayer and Bible study. Consider ways to infuse your family routines with spiritual meaning. For example, volunteering as a family at a local soup kitchen or homeless shelter can teach children the importance of compassion and service. Participating in community outreach programs provides opportunities to demonstrate Christian love in tangible ways, strengthening your family bond in the process. Simply acts of kindness, such as helping a neighbor or showing empathy to a friend in need, can embody the spirit of Christ and create a powerful legacy for your children.

Furthermore, making time for shared experiences of worship and praise is crucial. This isn't limited to attending church services; it can also include singing hymns at home, listening to inspirational music, or sharing inspiring stories of faith. This can cultivate an atmosphere of reverence and gratitude, nurturing the spiritual growth of each member. Even something as simple as lighting a candle before dinner and taking a moment of quiet reflection can create a sense of sacred space within your home.

Another powerful way to create a Christ-centered home is to cultivate an environment of forgiveness and reconciliation. Disagreements and conflicts are inevitable in any family, but how you handle them significantly impacts your home's atmosphere. Learning to forgive one another, modeling Christ's example of grace and mercy, is vital for maintaining healthy relationships. The power of prayer and biblical principles can help resolve disputes justly and lovingly, restoring harmony and peace. Open communication, active listening, and a willingness to compromise are essential tools in navigating conflict constructively.

Creating a Christ-centered home also means nurturing each family member's unique spiritual journey. Avoid imposing your faith or beliefs on others. Instead, create a space where questions and doubts are welcomed, encouraging open dialogue and spiritual exploration. Let children see your own struggle with faith, your personal doubts, and your ongoing journey with God. This authenticity creates a more honest and relatable environment for family members to discover their relationship with God. Consider incorporating spiritual disciplines into your daily routines. This might include setting aside time for personal reflection and meditation, journaling thoughts and feelings, or practicing mindfulness to improve focus and awareness. These practices not only promote personal spiritual growth but can also inspire family members to engage in these enriching activities together.

It's important to remember that building a Christ-centered home is an ongoing process, not a destination. There will be challenges and setbacks, moments of doubt and discouragement. But through perseverance, faith, and prayer, you can gradually create a loving, nurturing environment where faith is celebrated and shared, fostering a deep and meaningful connection with God and one another. It's a journey of continuous growth and learning, a testament to the transformative power of faith.

Think about the families you know who embody this spirit. Perhaps they consistently make time for family devotions, even if it's just for fifteen minutes before bed. Maybe they prioritize serving others as a family, volunteering their time and talents to those in need. Or maybe they simply create a home filled with laughter, love, and unwavering support, a haven where each member feels cherished and valued. These are all powerful examples of how faith can be woven into the everyday fabric of family life.

Consider families who have faced significant hardships—illness, financial struggles, the loss of a loved one—yet have emerged stronger and more united in their faith. These families demonstrate the resilience that comes from having Christ at the center. They found solace and strength in prayer, in their shared faith, and in their unwavering commitment to each other. These are not merely anecdotes but powerful examples of the transformative power of a Christ-centered home.

This journey of cultivating a Christ-centered home requires intentional effort and unwavering commitment. It's about making conscious choices to prioritize faith, to model Christ-like behavior, and to encourage spiritual growth within the family. It's about creating a space where love, grace, and forgiveness reign supreme, where every member feels safe, loved, and supported. It's about recognizing that building a strong family is a testament to the grace and mercy God offers us all.

Remember that this process is not about perfection; it's about progress. There will be days when you fall short, when you struggle to maintain the consistency you desire. But don't let this discourage you. Embrace imperfection, seek forgiveness, and strive to do better tomorrow. The journey is just as important as the destination. The goal is not to create a flawless, picture-perfect family but to build a loving, supportive community rooted in faith and strengthened by the unwavering love of God. And that is a journey worth embarking on. Let your home be a beacon of hope, a refuge of peace, and a testament to the transformative power of a life lived in Christ. Let the love of Christ be the guiding principle in all that you do, shaping your interactions, your decisions, and the very atmosphere of your home. This, more than anything else, will create a truly Christ-centered home.

## Overcoming Obstacles Through Faith

The unwavering faith that underpins a Christ-centered home isn't merely a Sunday ritual; it's the bedrock upon which the family navigates life's inevitable storms. It's the anchor that holds them steady amidst the turbulent waves of adversity, the compass guiding them towards calmer waters. Think of the biblical narrative of Joseph, sold into slavery by his brothers, betrayed, imprisoned, yet ultimately rising to become second in command in Egypt, saving his family from famine. His unwavering faith in God's plan, even amidst unspeakable hardship, is a testament to the transformative power of trust. His story isn't just a historical account; it's a living parable for families facing their own trials.

Joseph's journey highlights the crucial role of perspective. When faced with hardship, the inclination is often to focus on the immediate pain, the injustice, the seeming hopelessness of the situation. But faith encourages a different lens—a wider view that acknowledges the soereignty of God, even in the midst of suffering. It's a recognition that even in the darkest moments, God is working, shaping events, and ultimately orchestrating a greater good. Joseph didn't understand God's plan in the moment of his betrayal; he endured years of hardship, confusion, and despair.

Yet, his steadfast faith, his consistent reliance on God's promise, allowed him to persevere. His story reminds us that the path to fulfillment often winds through valleys of difficulty, that it is in these challenging moments that our faith is most profoundly tested and refined.

Consider the family of Job, a man described in scripture as blameless and upright. He suffered unimaginable loss—his livestock, his children, his health—yet, his response is a masterpiece of faith and submission. He didn't curse God, didn't question His justice. Instead, he clung to his belief in God's ultimate goodness, even when it seemed utterly absent from his own life. Job's wife urged him to curse God and die, a sentiment born from despair and a lack of understanding. But Job's unwavering faith, though tested to its limits, remained unbroken. His steadfastness wasn't about a lack of emotion; it was about a conscious choice to trust, to believe in a God whose ways are often beyond human comprehension. His story reminds us that faith doesn't negate suffering; it provides a framework for enduring it, a source of strength amidst the storm. The restoration that followed Job's suffering underscores the truth that God's blessings often follow trials, that perseverance in faith ultimately leads to renewal and redemption.

The trials faced by the Israelites during their journey through the wilderness offer another powerful example. Forty years of hardship, hunger, thirst, and constant threat of annihilation—a testing ground for their faith, a proving ground for their trust in God's promises.

Their complaints, their doubts, their moments of despair are all documented in scripture, a testament to the human struggle against uncertainty. Yet, throughout their arduous journey, God provided—manna from heaven, water from the rock, miraculous deliverance from their enemies. Their story underscores the enduring power of hope and perseverance, highlighting how faith, even when wavering, can sustain a community through incredibly challenging circumstances. It's a reminder that God's provision often appears in unexpected ways, at unexpected times. Their continued journey, despite their hardships, illustrates the necessity of enduring faith, of clinging to hope even when the future seems bleak.

These biblical examples demonstrate that faith isn't about

the absence of struggle, but the presence of unwavering trust, the belief that even in the darkest nights, God's light will eventually break through. It's about recognizing that God's plan is often larger than our own understanding, that His timing is perfect, even when it feels delayed or incomprehensible. It's about embracing the journey, both the triumphs and the tribulations, recognizing that each experience, good or bad, serves to deepen our faith, strengthen our resilience, and draw us closer to God.

Faith, therefore, is not passive acceptance of whatever life throws our way. It's an active engagement with God, a constant communication, a persistent seeking of His will and guidance. It's a continual dialogue between us and the Divine, a process of surrender and trust, of relinquishing our own control and embracing God's sovereignty. It involves prayer, both individual and collective, allowing the family to share their burdens, to seek strength and comfort in one another and in God's presence.The practice of prayer becomes a powerful tool in navigating obstacles. Through prayer, families can express their anxieties, their fears, their hopes, and their gratitude. It's a space for honest communication with God, where vulnerability is embraced and the weight of burdens is shared. It's in the stillness of prayer that peace can be found, where perspective can be gained, and where the strength to persevere is renewed.

The consistent practice of prayer, as a family, strengthens the bond between family members and reinforces their dependence on God's unwavering love and support.Furthermore, studying scripture, both individually and as a family, provides sustenance for the soul during difficult times. The scriptures offer guidance, comfort, and inspiration. They remind us of God's faithfulness throughout history, of His promises to His people, and of His enduring love. Reading scripture together as a family, discussing its relevance to their current situation, strengthens their understanding of God's plan and reinforces the principles of faith that guide their lives. It becomes a shared experience, a source of common understanding and mutual support.

The application of biblical principles in everyday life is crucial. The concept of forgiveness, as central to Christianity, plays a significant role in overcoming obstacles. Holding onto resentment, anger, and unforgiveness only adds to the burden. Forgiveness, both of ourselves and of others, is a powerful act of faith, a release of negativity that allows for healing and reconciliation.

Families that learn to forgive one another create a safe and supportive environment where love can flourish, even in the midst of conflict.

The practice of gratitude, too, is essential. In times of difficulty, it can be easy to focus solely on what is lacking, on what is going wrong. However, a conscious effort to acknowledge and appreciate even the small blessings can shift the perspective and foster a sense of hope. Expressing gratitude as a family, highlighting the positive aspects of their lives, strengthens their unity and reinforces their faith in God's goodness. Finally, faith isn't a magic wand that eliminates challenges; it's a source of strength and resilience that helps families navigate difficulties. It's about understanding that challenges are part of life, that they are opportunities for growth and for deepening faith. It's about maintaining a steadfast commitment to God's plan, even when that plan is unclear or painful.

It's about trusting that God's love is unwavering, His grace is sufficient, and His presence is constant, guiding and sustaining us through every storm. In the end, it is through this unwavering faith, this steadfast reliance on God's plan, that families find the strength to overcome obstacles and emerge stronger, their bonds deepened, their faith strengthened, and their commitment to one another renewed.

## The Power of Prayer in Family Life

The unwavering faith discussed earlier isn't just a passive belief; it's an active, vibrant force expressed most powerfully through prayer. Prayer isn't a mere ritualistic act, but a lifeline connecting our family to the divine source of strength, wisdom, and love. It's the very breath of a Christ-centered home, infusing every aspect of family life with a profound sense of purpose and unity. Think of it as the unseen glue holding the family together, strengthening bonds that might otherwise fray under the pressures of daily life.

Consider the family of Naomi, Ruth, and Boaz, a timeless example from the **Book of Ruth** . Their story, woven with threads of loss, loyalty, and unwavering faith, showcases the power of prayer implicitly. Though the text doesn't explicitly detail their prayer routines, their actions speak volumes about their reliance on a higher power. Naomi's lamentations were prayers of desperation and surrender, Ruth's unwavering devotion to her mother-in-law reflects a deep-seated faith, and Boaz's kindness and protection suggest a life lived in conscious acknowledgement of God's providence. Their journey, marked by hardship and uncertainty, ultimately culminates in blessing and restoration, underscoring the profound influence of faith, even unspoken, on their family
dynamics. Their story implicitly teaches us that even the silent prayers of a heart burdened with faith have transformative power.

Incorporating prayer into the daily rhythm of a family can seem daunting, especially for those unfamiliar with consistent prayer practices. Yet, the most effective prayers aren't necessarily long, eloquent pronouncements; they are honest, heartfelt expressions of need, gratitude, and surrender. Start small. A simple prayer before meals, a brief moment of quiet reflection before bedtime, or a shared prayer during a family gathering can collectively create a powerful atmosphere of faith. The key is consistency, not length. A five-minute prayer shared honestly every day is far more powerful than a rushed, thirty-minute prayer once a week.

Think of prayer as a conversation, not a monologue. Engage with God as you would with a trusted friend, expressing your joys, anxieties, and hopes. Share the burdens you carry, the victories you celebrate, and the uncertainties that weigh heavily on your hearts. Allow each family member, regardless of age, to participate. Children, especially, benefit from witnessing their parents model a life of prayer, learning to communicate directly with God from an early age.

Their prayers might be simple, yet they hold an unparalleled purity and innocence. Prayer, when practiced together, fosters an unparalleled intimacy within the family. It creates a sacred space where vulnerability is embraced, where honesty is valued, and where love finds fertile ground to blossom. During prayer, barriers crumble and hearts connect on a deeper level than words alone can ever express. Imagine the family gathered around, each individual sharing their personal concerns and praises, weaving together a tapestry of faith and mutual support. This shared experience cultivates empathy, compassion, and understanding, forging stronger bonds of love and respect. This isn't about creating a perfectly pious facade; it's about creating a genuine atmosphere of openness and mutual support in the presence of God.

Shared prayer becomes a powerful tool in resolving conflicts.Instead of letting disagreements escalate into bitter arguments, families can turn to prayer to seek God's guidance and wisdom. Praying together for understanding and forgiveness can dissolve resentment and pave the way for reconciliation. Learning to approach conflict from a place of prayer helps to shift perspectives, foster empathy, and replace anger with love. It provides a pathway for forgiveness and resolution, building resilience and strengthening the family unit. A simple prayer, asking for God's help to see the situation from another's perspective, can often be the catalyst for healing.

The power of prayer extends beyond the immediate family. It can be used as a means to pray for extended family, friends, and even for people the family has never met. This act of extending compassion and love beyond the immediate circle fosters a sense of unity and interconnectedness. It underscores the importance of shared humanity and highlights the expansive power of prayer to touch lives far and wide. Encouraging family members to pray forothers nurtures empathy, strengthens character, and fosters a sense of responsibility towards the wider community. Consider the example of a family facing a serious illness. Shared prayer becomes a powerful source of strength and comfort.

The family's faith, expressed through unified prayer, can provide solace during difficult times, offering a sense of hope and peace amidst suffering. It can also create a sense of community and shared purpose, bringing the family closer together and fostering a profound sense of mutual support. The consistent act of praying together acts as a visible manifestation of their collective faith, strengthening their bonds and fortifying their resilience against adversity.

Let's illustrate this with a practical example. The Johnson family, a seemingly ordinary family, faced an extraordinary challenge. Their teenage daughter, Beautiful Angle, was diagnosed with a severe illness. The uncertainty and fear were overwhelming. However, the Johnsons had long established a habit of daily family prayer. In this crisis, their shared faith became their lifeline. They prayed together every night, each member sharing their fears, hopes, and anxieties.

They prayed for Beautiful Angle's healing, for strength to

endure, and for peace in the face of uncertainty. The consistent prayer didn't magically cure Beautiful Angle, but it provided them with an unwavering sense of hope and resilience. It fostered an extraordinary level of intimacy and mutual support, strengthening their family bond in a way that words alone cannot describe. They learned to lean on each other, relying on their faith and their shared prayer as their unwavering anchor.

Another example is the Miller family, a family known for their frequent disagreements. Conflict was commonplace, with frustration brewing over almost every issue. But a new pastor at their church encouraged the practice of daily family prayer. Initially, the practice felt forced and awkward. Yet, as they persisted, they discovered something remarkable. Their prayers became a space for honest communication, for expressing vulnerabilities, and for seeking forgiveness. As they prayed together, they began to see each other differently, understanding each other's needs and struggles.

Their conflicts didn't vanish overnight, but the approach to those conflicts fundamentally changed. Prayer became a pathway to empathy, transforming their relationships and fostering a deeper connection. The constant prayer became a tangible expression of their commitment to each other and to God. Their disagreements eventually lessened, replaced by greater understanding and mutual respect.

Finally, the power of prayer in family life isn't about achieving a picture-perfect family, devoid of conflict or struggle. It's about cultivating a family that navigates challenges, resolves conflicts, and celebrates joys with faith as its guiding principle. It's about creating a home where God's presence is palpable, where love reigns supreme, and where prayer acts as the very heartbeat of the family. Remember, prayer isn't a magic formula, but a powerful tool to connect with God and with each other, drawing strength from the divine source and building a home founded on faith, love, and unwavering commitment. It's about creating a haven of peace and strength, a testament to the transformative power of prayer in the very core of family life. It's a journey, not a destination, and the consistent effort invested will yield immeasurable blessings. The reward isn't just a harmonious family; it's a family forged in faith, resilient in adversity, and deeply rooted in the love of God.

## Finding Rest in Gods Sovereignty

The relentless pursuit of perfection, the constant striving to achieve more, to be more, to *do* more—this is a familiar rhythm for many of us, isn't it? We chase after milestones, juggle responsibilities, and often find ourselves exhausted, yet still feeling unfulfilled. We yearn for rest, for peace, but the relentless demands of life seem to perpetually outpace our capacity. This pursuit, however, often leads us down a path of anxiety and frustration, a path that diverges sharply from the peace and contentment that God promises. True rest, profound peace, isn't found in our tireless efforts, but in a surrender of control, a conscious act of yielding to God's sovereign plan.

Consider the parable of the sower in **Matthew 13** . The seed represents the word of God, sown in different soils – some rocky, some thorny, some good. The seeds that fell on good soil sprouted and bore fruit, while those in less fertile ground withered or were choked. The parable isn't simply about the reception of God's word; it's a metaphor for our hearts, our capacity to receive His grace and allow it to flourish. When we relentlessly strive, clinging tightly to our own plans and timelines, we become like the rocky or thorny ground—unable to fully receive the nourishment of God's love and guidance. We become so focused on what *we* want to achieve that we miss the subtle whispers of God's direction, the gentle nudges towards His perfect plan.

The beauty of God's sovereignty is that it doesn't negate our efforts; rather, it frames them within a larger, more meaningful context. It's not about passive resignation, but an active trust. It's about understanding that God's plan is far greater, far more encompassing, than anything we could ever conceive on our own. When we surrender our anxieties, our fears, and our desperate need to control outcomes, we create space for God to work in miraculous ways. We open ourselves to the possibility of unexpected blessings, unforeseen opportunities, and a joy that surpasses our wildest dreams.

This surrender, this letting go, isn't easy. It requires a profound humility, a willingness to acknowledge our limitations and admit that we don't always have the answers. It demands faith – a deep and unwavering trust in a God who loves us unconditionally and who has a perfect plan for our lives, even when that plan doesn't look like what we expected. This faith isn't simply a feeling; it's a decision, a commitment to trust in God's wisdom and guidance, even amidst uncertainty and adversity. This can involve actively choosing to relinquish control in specific areas, consciously handing over our worries and concerns to God through prayer and meditation.

Think about your own life. Are there areas where you're struggling to let go of control? Perhaps it's your children's future, your financial stability, or your health. These are natural concerns, but clinging to control only amplifies our anxiety and diminishes our ability to experience peace. Letting go isn't about neglecting responsibility; it's about trusting that God is working even when we can't see it. It's about aligning ourselves with His will, surrendering our own limited perspectives and embracing His infinite wisdom. Consider **Psalm 46:10** : *"Be still, and know that I am God."* This isn't a passive command; it's an invitation to a transformative experience. It's a call to silence the clamor of our own anxieties and to find stillness in the presence of God. In this stillness, we can hear His voice, receive His guidance, and find the rest our souls desperately crave. This stillness is not the absence of activity; rather, it's a state of inner peace, a deep-seated trust in God's plan, that allows us to navigate the complexities of life with grace and confidence.

Within the context of family life, this surrender to God's sovereignty is crucial. The pressures of raising children, managing a household, and balancing work and family can be overwhelming. When we try to control every aspect of our family's life, we become burdened by a weight that we were never intended to bear. Surrendering to God's plan allows us to approach family life with a renewed sense of perspective, acknowledging that He is the ultimate provider, protector, and guide. Imagine a family constantly embroiled in conflict, struggling with unresolved issues, and lacking a shared sense of purpose. Often, this stems from a lack of trust—not just in each other, but in God's ability to work through their challenges. When we place our faith in God's sovereignty, we release the burden of trying to fix everything ourselves, acknowledging that He is the source of healing, reconciliation, and strength. We can approach conflict with a renewed spirit of humility, seeking guidance from Him and trusting in His timing and wisdom.

Let's consider the example of a family facing financial hardship. Instead of succumbing to fear and anxiety, they can choose to trust in God's provision. This isn't a guarantee of sudden wealth; it's a faith-filled response that acknowledges God's sovereignty over their circumstances. They might seek guidance through prayer, rely on the support of their community, and explore creative solutions with trust in God's guidance. Their actions might include tightening their budgets, seeking additional work, or relying on the generosity of others, but their underlying approach is rooted in faith. They will endure, adapting and trusting in God's ultimate provision. The outcome may not be immediate relief, but a peace that surpasses understanding.

Similarly, consider a family dealing with a child's health crisis. The fear, the uncertainty, the overwhelming emotions —these are all understandable. However, surrendering to God's sovereignty doesn't mean passively accepting whatever happens. It means facing the challenge with faith, seeking medical help, and praying for healing and strength. It means entrusting the outcome to God's hands, trusting that He will work through their circumstances, offering comfort, strength and maybe even healing. The focus shifts from a desperate struggle for control to a quiet confidence in God's love and power.

The beauty of surrendering to God's sovereignty is that it doesn't diminish our efforts or responsibilities. On the contrary, it enhances them. When we release our anxieties and trust in God's plan, we're empowered to act with greater clarity, focus, and peace. We can work towards our goals with less pressure, knowing that God is guiding our steps and that even setbacks are part of His larger plan.

The journey of surrender is not a single event but a continuous process. It's a daily choice to relinquish control and trust in God's wisdom. It requires humility, patience, and a willingness to be surprised by God's ways. It often involves wrestling with doubt, questioning, and uncertainty, but the reward is a peace that transcends understanding, a joy that defies the storms of life, and a strength that sustains us through even the toughest trials. It's a pathway to a deeply satisfying life, a life rooted in the unshakeable foundation of God's love and unwavering faithfulness. The journey is worth it. The rest is worth fighting for. The peace is worth embracing.

## Chapter2: Communication: The Bridge to Understanding

-Open Communication The Cornerstone of Healthy Relalationships

-Active Listening Hearing Beyond Words

-Resolving Conflicts Through Godly Communication

-Forgiveness A Cornerstone of Healthy Communicat

-Non-violent Communication Techniques

## Open Communication The Cornerstone of Healthy Relationships

Open communication isn't merely about exchanging words; it's the lifeblood of any healthy relationship, particularly within the family unit. Think of a family as a finely tuned orchestra. Each member plays a unique instrument, contributing to the overall harmony. But without a conductor – clear, open communication – the music becomes discordant, a cacophony of misunderstood notes. In a family context, this "conductor" ensures everyone feels heard, understood, and valued. The Bible consistently emphasizes the importance of speaking truth in love ( **Ephesians 4:15** ), a principle that forms the bedrock of healthy communication.

Consider the story of the prodigal son in **Luke 15** . The son's eventual return was preceded by a deep, honest confession of his mistakes. His father, in turn, didn't react with anger or judgment but with overwhelming love and forgiveness. This open communication, marked by honesty and compassion, ultimately restored their broken relationship. This illustrates the power of vulnerability in communication – the willingness to share our fears, doubts, and mistakes without fear of judgment or rejection.

Active listening is a crucial component of open communication. It's more than just hearing the words; it's about truly understanding the speaker's emotions, intentions, and perspective. It involves paying close attention not only to the verbal message but also to the nonverbal cues – body language, tone of voice, and facial expressions. When we actively listen, we create a safe space for others to express themselves fully, knowing their words will be received with empathy and understanding. This isn't always easy; we are often distracted by our own thoughts and concerns, making it challenging to focus entirely on the speaker. However, mastering this skill is transformative.Imagine a scenario where a teenage child is struggling with academic pressure and feeling overwhelmed. If their parent engages in active listening, truly hearing the child's anxieties and frustrations, it fosters a sense of trust and support. The parent isn't just offering solutions; they are validating the child's feelings, allowing them to feel seen and understood. This approach significantly strengthens the parent-child bond and encourages open dialogue in the future. Contrast this with a parent who dismisses the child's concerns, focusing instead on lecturing or offering unsolicited advice. This approach shuts down communication, creating distance and resentment.

Expressing feelings constructively is another cornerstone of open communication. This doesn't mean venting anger or unleashing harsh criticism. Instead, it involves articulating our needs and emotions in a calm, respectful manner, using "I" statements to avoid blaming or accusing others. For example, instead of saying, "You always leave the dishes dirty," a more constructive approach would be, "I feel frustrated when the dishes are left unwashed because it adds to my workload." This approach shifts the focus from blame to personal feelings, making the message more receptive.

Empathy, the ability to understand and share the feelings of another, is crucial for effective communication. Putting ourselves in another person's shoes, considering their perspective, even if we don't agree with it, fosters understanding and connection. This doesn't mean we condone harmful behaviors; it simply means we strive to comprehend the underlying reasons behind those behaviors, recognizing that people often act out of pain, fear, or insecurity. Within the family, empathy bridges gaps, fostering compassion and forgiveness.

The Bible frequently underscores the importance of empathy. Jesus, in his interactions with others, consistently demonstrated remarkable empathy, understanding their needs and responding with compassion. His interactions with the woman at the well ( **John 4** ) exemplifies this beautifully. He didn't judge her, but instead engaged her with kindness and understanding, ultimately leading her to faith. This empathy-driven approach forms the basis for many of the parables, highlighting the importance of understanding and compassion in our interactions with others.

Effective communication within a family also extends to handling conflict. Disagreements are inevitable, but how we address them shapes the overall health of the relationship. Avoiding conflict is not a solution; it allows resentment and misunderstanding to fester. Instead, creating a safe space to discuss disagreements openly and honestly is vital. This requires establishing ground rules: no name-calling, no personal attacks, and a commitment to listening to each other's perspectives before offering solutions.

Consider a family dealing with a conflict over a significant life decision, such as a child's choice of college. Open communication would involve each family member expressing their feelings and concerns calmly and respectfully, actively listening to others, and seeking a compromise that considers everyone's needs.

This process might involve several discussions, requiring patience and a willingness to understand different viewpoints. The goal isn't necessarily to achieve unanimous agreement; it's to navigate the conflict constructively, maintaining respect and understanding throughout the process. This commitment to open communication helps to resolve the immediate issue and strengthen family bonds in the long run.

Furthermore, forgiveness is an indispensable aspect of healthy communication. Holding onto resentment and anger poisons relationships, creating distance and bitterness. Forgiveness isn't condoning wrong actions; it's a conscious decision to release the pain and anger, allowing healing to begin. This process isn't easy, but it's essential for maintaining healthy relationships. The Bible repeatedly emphasizes the importance of forgiveness, both from God towards us and from us towards others ( **Matthew 6:14-15** ). Forgiving doesn't mean forgetting; it means choosing to let go of the bitterness and resentment that can destroy relationships.

Think of a scenario where a sibling has hurt another. Choosing forgiveness doesn't erase the hurt, but it allows the injured sibling to move forward, restoring the relationship and preventing the hurt from festering. The path to forgiveness often involves empathy, understanding the reasons behind the hurtful actions, and choosing to extend grace rather than judgment. This process can be facilitated through open, honest conversations where both parties express their feelings and work towards reconciliation.

Finally, the use of non-violent communication techniques can significantly improve the quality of family interactions. This approach involves expressing needs and feelings without resorting to blame, criticism, or judgment. It focuses on conveying our message clearly and respectfully, emphasizing empathy and understanding. This approach, inspired by principles of compassion and respect, creates a safe space for open communication and helps to prevent conflicts from escalating. Learning these techniques empowers us to navigate family dynamics more effectively, resulting in stronger and more fulfilling relationships.

In conclusion, open communication is not merely a skill; it's a spiritual discipline that strengthens the bonds within the family. It requires intentionality, effort, and a commitment to empathy, active listening, constructive expression, forgiveness, and the skillful use of non-violent communication. By embracing these principles, families can create a nurturing environment where each member feels heard, understood, and loved, building relationships that stand the test of time and reflect the love and grace found in Christ himself. The journey may have its challenges, but the rewards – a family united in love and understanding – are immeasurable.

## Active Listening Hearing Beyond Words

Active listening. The phrase itself sounds simple enough, almost mundane. Yet, the true art of hearing beyond the words, of truly understanding the heart behind the spoken message, is a skill often overlooked, particularly within the demanding landscape of family life. We often fall into the trap of passive listening, where our minds wander, preoccupied with our own thoughts and responses, while another person pours out their heart. This isn't intentional cruelty; it's a byproduct of our busy lives, a lack of practice in a skill that deserves careful cultivation. Think of the parable of the sower in **Matthew 13** .

The seed, representing God's word, falls on different types of soil, each representing a different type of listener. Some listen passively, their hearts hardened like rocky ground; the word bounces off, failing to take root. Others hear the word, but the anxieties and cares of this world choke the life out of it, preventing growth. True
understanding, the rich soil that nurtures the seed of
communication, requires active listening – a conscious decision to fully engage with what is being communicated.

Passive listening is characterized by a lack of engagement. We might nod occasionally, offer a noncommittal "uh-huh," but our attention remains elsewhere. Our minds are already formulating our replies, our focus on what *we* will say next, rather than truly grasping what is being said *to* us. This can lead to misunderstandings, hurt feelings, and the erosion of trust. Imagine a child confiding in a parent about a schoolyard bully, only to be met with a distracted "Tell me later, honey, I'm on a call." The message received isn't simply that the parent is busy; it's that the child's feelings aren't a priority in that moment. This seemingly small act can have profound consequences, sowing seeds of doubt and in security.

Active listening, in contrast, is a conscious effort to fully comprehend both the verbal and nonverbal cues of the speaker. It's about understanding not just the words themselves, but the emotions, anxieties, and underlying needs expressed through tone of voice, body language, and facial expressions. It requires setting aside our own preconceptions and agendas, focusing instead on the speaker's perspective. It's about giving the speaker our undivided attention, creating a safe space where they feel heard, validated, and understood. Consider the example of the Good Samaritan ( **Luke 10** ). The priest and Levite saw the injured man, but they didn't actively listen to his silent plea for help. Their hearts were closed to his need; they moved on, focusing on their own priorities. The Samaritan, however, stopped and actively listened, not only to the man's implicit cry for help but also to the promptings of his own heart.

How do we cultivate this essential skill of active listening? It begins with intentionality. Before engaging in a conversation, particularly with a family member, consciously make the decision to listen fully. Put aside distractions – turn off the TV, put down your phone, and create a space where you can give your undivided attention. This act alone signals respect and value to the speaker.

Then, focus on observing nonverbal cues. Are they fidgeting? Is their voice trembling? Do their eyes show sadness, anxiety, or anger? Nonverbal cues often speak volumes, offering crucial insights into the speaker's emotional state. A furrowed brow might suggest frustration; averted eyes could indicate shyness or discomfort. Paying attention to these nonverbal cues demonstrates that you are not only hearing their words but also feeling their emotions. This empathetic engagement deepens the connection and fosters trust.

Next, use verbal and nonverbal affirmations to show your

engagement. Simple phrases such as, "I hear you," "Tell me more," or "That must have been difficult," can go a long way in reassuring the speaker that you are listening and empathizing with their experience. Nodding your head, maintaining eye contact (without staring intensely, which can be intimidating), and mirroring their body language subtly (not mimicking, but reflecting their posture in a relaxed way) shows your engagement and creates a sense of connection. These small gestures speak louder than words. Another critical aspect of active listening is paraphrasing and summarizing. Restating what you've heard in your own words demonstrates your understanding and provides the speaker with an opportunity to clarify or correct any misinterpretations.

For example, if your child says, "School is terrible," instead of immediately launching into advice, try paraphrasing: "So, it sounds like you're feeling really frustrated and unhappy about something at school. Can you tell me more?" This shows that you're listening carefully and that you want to understand their perspective fully.

Furthermore, active listening requires the ability to resist interrupting. It's a common human tendency to interrupt when we think we know what someone is going to say, or when we have a strong urge to share our own perspective. However, interrupting breaks the flow of communication and makes the speaker feel unheard. Train yourself to pause before responding, giving the speaker ample opportunity to fully express themselves. Practice the art of silence, allowing for the natural pauses in conversation, allowing the speaker the time and space they need to reveal the depths of their heart.

Active listening isn't a passive activity; it's an active engagement of your mind, body, and spirit. It is an act of love, mirroring God's own love for us. He patiently listens to our prayers, our anxieties, our praises, without interruption or judgment. He sees our hearts, understands our weaknesses, and offers His grace and forgiveness. As we strive to emulate Him in our family relationships, practicing active listening becomes a powerful tool for building stronger, healthier, and more loving bonds.

Consider the story of David and Jonathan. Their relationship was built on deep mutual trust and understanding.

They actively listened to each other's concerns and hopes, supporting each other through thick and thin. Their friendship stands as a testament to the power of genuine communication and mutual respect. Jonathan didn't just hear David's words; he felt his fears, celebrated his triumphs, and stood by him through his darkest hours. In contrast, think about situations where active listening has failed. Perhaps a heated argument escalated because each person was too busy formulating their rebuttal to fully hear the other's perspective.

Or maybe a parent missed a crucial signal of distress from a child, leading to later regret and strained relationship. These failures highlight the importance of intentional, active listening. It's a practice that requires patience, empathy, and a willingness to set aside our own agendas, to truly see and understand the person before us. It's a practice rooted in love, compassion, and understanding.

Finally, remember that active listening is not about fixing problems or offering solutions immediately. Sometimes, people just need to be heard. They need a space to vent their frustrations, to share their anxieties, to be understood. Offer empathy, validation, and support. Your presence alone, your active listening, can be a powerful balm to a hurting heart. This act of listening is itself a powerful form of love, reflecting the unconditional love of God. As we strive to create families that reflect the love and harmony found in the kingdom of God, the ability to actively listen, to truly hear beyond the words, becomes not only a skill but a cornerstone of our relationships. It is a bridge to understanding, a pathway to healing, and a testament to the love that binds us together.

## Resolving Conflicts Through Godly Communication

Building upon the foundation of active listening, we now move to the crucial element of resolving conflict through godly communication. It's a common misconception that disagreements are inherently negative. In reality, conflict, when handled constructively, can serve as a catalyst for deeper understanding and stronger bonds. The key lies not in avoiding conflict, but in navigating it with wisdom and grace, mirroring the love and forgiveness found in Christ's teachings.The Bible offers a wealth of guidance on conflict resolution. Consider the parable of the unforgiving servant in **Matthew 18:21-35** .

This parable underscores the importance of forgiveness, not just as a pious act, but as an essential component of healthy relationships. Holding onto resentment and bitterness poisons the wellspring of love, creating distance and hindering the growth of genuine connection. Just as the servant who received forgiveness failed to extend it to others, we too risk jeopardizing our relationships by refusing to forgive. Forgiveness, however, doesn't mean condoning harmful behavior. It means releasing the grip of anger and resentment, choosing love and reconciliation.

Our journey towards resolving conflict begins with a posture of humility. **Proverbs 15:1** reminds us, *"A soft answer turns away wrath, but a harsh word stirs up anger."* Approaching a conflict with a gentle spirit, acknowledging our own imperfections and potential contribution to the disagreement, sets the stage for productive dialogue. This doesn't imply weakness; it's a demonstration of strength—the strength to admit fault, the strength to seek reconciliation, the strength to model the humility of Christ.

The next step involves seeking to understand the other person's perspective, actively listening, not to formulate a rebuttal, but to truly grasp their feelings and concerns. Often, conflicts arise from miscommunication, from differing interpretations of events, or from unmet needs. By patiently listening, we can discern the root cause of the conflict, moving beyond surface-level arguments to address the underlying issues. This requires empathy—the ability to step into another person's shoes, to see the world through their eyes. Remember the Golden Rule: Treat others as you would want to be treated ( **Matthew 7:12** ).

Once we understand each other's perspectives, we can begin to find common ground. This often involves compromise, a willingness to set aside our own desires for the sake of unity. Compromise isn't about surrendering our values; it's about finding mutually acceptable solutions that honor God and strengthen the relationship. It's about seeking a win-win scenario, not a win-lose scenario. This mirrors God's own approach to us; He compromises in His love for us, demonstrating patience and compassion even when we fall short.

**Ephesians 4:26-27** provides further instruction: *"In your anger do not sin: Do not let the sun go down while you are still angry, and do not give the devil a foothold."* These verses emphasize the importance of timely resolution. Allowing anger to fester only exacerbates the conflict, creating deeper wounds and hindering reconciliation. Addressing disagreements promptly prevents minor issues from escalating into major crises. This immediate attention to conflict models Christ's prompt and unwavering love, always ready to heal and restore.

Let's explore a real-life scenario. Imagine a family dealing with a conflict over financial decisions. One spouse feels the family is spending too much money on non-essentials, while the other feels restricted and believes their needs are not being met. Using godly communication, they begin by actively listening to each other's concerns, validating each other's feelings. The spouse who feels restricted shares their feelings of insecurity and lack of autonomy, while the other spouse explains their concerns about financial stability and the importance of planning for the future. Through this shared understanding, they find common ground, compromising on a budget that addresses both their needs while aligning with their shared values. This resolution involves prayerful consideration, seeking God's wisdom and guidance in their financial choices.

Another example could involve sibling rivalry. Two children constantly argue over toys and attention. Instead of simply reprimanding them, parents can use godly communication to help them understand each other's perspectives. They can guide the children to actively listen, to express their feelings without resorting to insults or accusations. The parents can facilitate a process of compromise, helping the siblings find ways to share resources and resolve conflicts fairly. This involves teaching them the value of empathy, reminding them of the importance of loving each other as Christ loves us.

Consider a marriage struggling with communication breakdowns. Perhaps one spouse feels unheard and unappreciated, while the other feels overwhelmed and misunderstood. Through prayerful communication, both spouses can begin to share their vulnerabilities and unmet needs. This requires setting aside time for focused and uninterrupted conversation, a space free from distractions and interruptions. Active listening becomes essential here, ensuring that each partner feels genuinely heard and validated. The goal is not to win the argument but to find common ground, to build a stronger bond based on mutual respect and understanding. Forgiveness plays a crucial role; past hurts need to be addressed and forgiven for healing to occur. The commitment to continue improving communication and to seek God's guidance in their marriage becomes a pivotal aspect of this process.

Through these scenarios, we see how godly communication —rooted in active listening, empathy, humility, compromise, and forgiveness—can transform conflict into an opportunity for growth and reconciliation. It is a powerful tool for building strong, healthy relationships that reflect the love and grace of God.

The process is not always easy, requiring patience, perseverance, and a willingness to set aside our own pride. But the rewards—deeper understanding, stronger bonds, and a greater reflection of God's love in our families—are immeasurable. The journey of resolving conflicts through godly communication is a continuous process, requiring ongoing practice and a commitment to prioritizing love and unity above all else. It's a journey of faith, trusting in God's guidance and His transformative power to mend broken relationships and create harmony within our families and beyond. Remember, the goal isn't simply to resolve the conflict, but to strengthen the relationship, building a foundation of trust and love that honors God and blesses all involved.

This approach to conflict resolution, modeled on Christ's teachings and demonstrated through practical application, provides a pathway towards fulfilling the biblical mandate of building strong families rooted in faith, love, and understanding. It's a testament to the enduring power of grace and the transformative potential of godly communication. The very act of seeking reconciliation reflects God's own heart—a heart overflowing with forgiveness, compassion, and unconditional love. By embracing these principles, we not only resolve conflicts but also cultivate an environment where love thrives and families flourish.

## Forgiveness A Cornerstone of Healthy Communication

Forgiveness isn't merely a passive act of letting go; it's an active choice, a powerful decision that unlocks healing and reconciliation. It's a cornerstone of healthy communication, a bridge that spans the chasms of hurt and resentment, leading to restored relationships and a stronger sense of family unity. Think of it as the mortar that holds the bricks of communication together, ensuring a strong and lasting structure. Without forgiveness, even the most heartfelt words can fall flat, leaving a lingering bitterness that poisons the well of communication.

The Bible is replete with examples of forgiveness, its transformative power woven into the very fabric of scripture. Consider the parable of the unforgiving servant in **Matthew 18:21-35** . This parable vividly illustrates the devastating consequences of withholding forgiveness. The servant, who had been forgiven an immense debt, refused to forgive a much smaller debt owed to him. This lack of compassion brought swift and severe judgment. This parable doesn't simply tell us to forgive; it underscores the profound spiritual implications of holding onto resentment. Forgiving others, as Jesus emphasized, is intrinsically linked to our own relationship with God. When we refuse to forgive, we are, in essence, rejecting the very grace and mercy that has been freely given to us.

Forgiveness, however, is not a simple formula; it's a journey, often a long and arduous one. It involves a willingness to confront our own emotions, to acknowledge the pain we've endured, and to consciously choose to release the burden of resentment. It's about shifting our perspective, recognizing that our capacity to forgive isn't dependent on the other person's repentance or remorse. We forgive not because they deserve it, but because we need to be free.

Holding onto anger and bitterness only serves to poison our

own hearts, hindering our emotional well-being and preventing us from experiencing the peace and joy that God intends for us. Forgiving others begins with acknowledging our own human frailty. We are all flawed, prone to making mistakes, and capable of causing hurt. Recognizing this inherent imperfection in ourselves makes it easier to extend compassion and understanding towards those who have wronged us. Remember, empathy is the cornerstone of forgiveness.

Try to understand the other person's perspective, their motivations, and the circumstances that led to their actions.This doesn't mean condoning their behavior, but it does mean seeking to understand the roots of their actions, thereby gaining a deeper perspective and a greater capacity for compassion.The process of forgiving someone is rarely instantaneous; it's often a gradual unfolding, a progression from anger and hurt to acceptance and peace. It may involve several stages. Initially, there's the acknowledgement of the hurt— allowing ourselves to feel the pain without judgment.

Then, there's a conscious decision to let go of the anger and resentment, releasing the hold it has on our hearts and minds. This doesn't necessarily mean that we forget what happened, but rather that we choose not to allow it to continue to define or control our lives. Finally, there's the active choice to forgive, extending compassion and grace to the person who has hurt us. This is not about minimizing the offense, but about releasing the weight of unforgiveness.

Asking for forgiveness is equally crucial. It's an act of humility, a recognition of our own failings and a willingness to seek reconciliation. It takes courage to admit we've made a mistake, to acknowledge the hurt we've caused, and to humbly ask for forgiveness. But it's a vital step in restoring relationships and building trust. When we ask for forgiveness, we are not only seeking reconciliation with the other person, but we're also demonstrating a willingness to learn and grow.

However, asking for forgiveness doesn't guarantee it will be granted. The other person may need time to process their feelings, or they may not be ready to forgive. Respect their process; continue to show genuine remorse and allow them the space they need. The primary focus of asking for forgiveness is not in obtaining the forgiveness, but in taking responsibility for your actions and
showing the other person that you value the relationship enough to demonstrate genuine repentance.

Let's explore some real-life examples to illustrate the practical application of forgiveness within families.

Consider a family where a sibling betrayed a trust, leading to intense feelings of betrayal and anger. The path to healing might involve a heart-to-heart conversation, the betrayed sibling expressing their hurt honestly and openly, while the sibling who caused the hurt acknowledges their wrongdoing and genuinely expresses remorse. The process of forgiveness may take time, perhaps involving a series of conversations, acts of kindness, and a commitment to rebuilding trust. The goal isn't to erase the memory of the offense, but to allow it to become a catalyst for growth and deeper understanding.

Forgiveness, in this context, is not about condoning the behavior, but about choosing to release the bitterness and resentment it engendered.Another scenario might involve parents who had a strained relationship with their adult children due to unresolved conflicts. Perhaps unresolved issues from the past continued to cause friction. Healing could involve the parents acknowledging their role in the conflict, perhaps expressing regret for any past hurts, and the children in turn, extending forgiveness for any past actions.

This process might involve seeking professional guidance, attending family therapy, or engaging in deep prayer and reflection.Forgiveness, in this scenario, becomes the cornerstone of rebuilding a stronger, healthier relationship, one that transcends past hurts and allows for a more fulfilling future. Furthermore, consider the impact of unforgiveness on future generations. When parents carry unresolved hurts and resentments, they can inadvertently pass these down to their children, creating cycles of conflict and dysfunction. Children who witness unresolved conflicts may learn unhealthy coping mechanisms, affecting their own relationships in adulthood. Forgiveness, therefore, isn't just essential for individual well-being; it is also vital for the health and well-being of the family as a whole. It breaks the cycle of negativity, promoting an environment of healing and growth.

The process of forgiveness often requires seeking guidance and support. Prayer, meditation, and reflection can provide comfort, solace, and insight. Seeking professional help from a counselor or therapist is often beneficial, especially when dealing with deep-seated hurts or complex family dynamics. Support groups can provide a sense of community and shared understanding, offering encouragement and practical strategies for navigating the path toward forgiveness. Remember, seeking help isn't a sign of weakness, but rather a testament to your courage and commitment to healing.

Scripture offers a wealth of guidance on the subject of forgiveness. **Colossians 3:13** reminds us to "bear with each other and forgive one another if any of you has a grievance against someone. Forgive as the Lord forgave you." **Ephesians 4:32** encourages us to be "kind and compassionate to one another, forgiving each other, just as in Christ God forgave you." These verses underscore the reciprocal nature of forgiveness—we are to forgive as we have been forgiven.

Finally, the journey of forgiveness is not a solo endeavor. It often requires the participation and support of those involved.

It's about a shared commitment to healing and reconciliation, recognizing the interconnectedness of our lives and the profound impact our actions have on others. It's a journey undertaken with humility, grace, and unwavering faith in God's restorative power. Remember, forgiveness isn't about forgetting; it's about releasing the power that the hurt has over you.

It's about choosing healing over bitterness, choosing love over resentment, choosing unity over division. It is about recognizing that true freedom lies not in holding on to the past, but in releasing it into the hands of a loving and forgiving God.

Forgiveness, therefore, is not just an important aspect of healthy communication; it is a vital ingredient in building strong, loving, and lasting relationships. It is a testament to the transformative power of grace, mirroring the boundless love and forgiveness of God himself, allowing families to flourish and truly reflect His glory.

## Nonviolent Communication Techniques

Building upon the foundation of forgiveness, we now turn to the practical application of non-violent communication within the family unit. This isn't about suppressing emotions or pretending disagreements don't exist; rather, it's about learning to express ourselves honestly and respectfully, fostering an environment where vulnerability is embraced and conflict is approached as an opportunity for growth and deeper understanding, mirroring God's own patient and loving approach to us.

The core of non-violent communication (NVC), often referred to as compassionate communication, lies in understanding our own needs and the needs of others.Too often, conflicts arise not from inherently malicious intentions, but from a misunderstanding of underlying needs. A child's tantrum, for example, might stem not from a desire to defy parental authority, but from a deep-seated need for attention, security, or understanding. Similarly, a marital dispute might originate not from inherent incompatibility, but from unmet needs for appreciation, connection, or autonomy.

Recognizing these underlying needs is the first crucial step. NVC provides a framework for this self-awareness, encouraging us to move beyond the surface level of complaints and accusations to explore the deeper emotional landscape. Instead of saying, "You never help with the chores!", a more effective approach might be, "I feel over  whelmed when the house is messy, and I need help to feel supported and less stressed." Notice the shift: from blame ("You never...") to a description of feeling ("I feel overwhelmed...") and an articulation of the underlying need ("I need help..."). This subtle change transforms the communication from an attack to a request for support.

This framework involves four key components: observations, feelings, needs, and requests. Let's break each one down:

**Observations:** This step emphasizes separating facts from interpretations. Instead of saying, "You're always late," which is an interpretation, a more objective observation would be, "You arrived fifteen minutes late for dinner tonight." The difference may seem minor, but it drastically reduces defensiveness. The aim is to describe the situation without judgment or emotional coloring. Think of it as presenting the raw data, allowing the other person to understand the situation clearly before addressing the emotional response. Practice this with everyday scenarios – recounting an event without judgment or opinion. This disciplined approach sharpens our observational skills and helps create a more accurate and peaceful communication.

**Feelings:** After making an observation, express your feelings. This is about owning your emotions, connecting them to the situation, and avoiding vague statements like "I feel bad." Instead, be specific. "When you arrived late, I felt anxious because I'd prepared a special meal and worried that it would get cold, and I felt disappointed that our planned evening together was disrupted." This clear articulation of feelings removes the ambiguity and allows for a more genuine connection. Consider a wide range of feeling words: hurt, disappointed, frustrated, anxious, overwhelmed, lonely, joyful, grateful, excited, peaceful. The richer your emotional vocabulary, the more nuanced your communication becomes.

**Needs:** This is where the heart of NVC lies – identifying the underlying needs that fuel our feelings. In the example above, the underlying need is likely a need for consideration, respect, connection, and shared quality time. Identifying needs helps shift the focus from blaming to understanding the core issue. Are you longing for connection, respect, security, autonomy, or something else? Exploring your needs opens up opportunities for creative solutions that address everyone's fundamental requirements. Remember the list of needs is expansive, and understanding your personal needs is a journey of self-discovery.

**Requests:** Finally, make a clear and concrete request. Instead of demanding, "You need to be on time," a request might be, "Could you please make an effort to be on time for dinner next time? I'd really appreciate it, and it would help me feel less stressed." A request is always a choice; the other person is free to accept or decline without guilt or judgment. This preserves respect and allows for genuine collaboration in finding mutually agreeable solutions. Let's consider another example: a teenager who slams their bedroom door after a disagreement with a parent. Instead of reacting with anger, the parent could use NVC. They might say: "I observed you slamming your door. When I saw that, I felt worried and concerned about you. I need to feel connected with you and understand how you're doing. Could we talk about this later
tonight?"This response acknowledges the behavior without judgment, expresses the parent's feelings and underlying needs, and offers a concrete request for dialogue.

Applying NVC requires practice and patience. It's a journey, not a destination. Initially, it might feel awkward or unnatural, but with consistent effort, it becomes a powerful tool for resolving conflicts and building stronger relationships. Remember, the goal is not to avoid conflict entirely, but to navigate it with empathy,
understanding, and respect, guided by the principles of love and forgiveness that form the bedrock of our faith. Just as God patiently works with us, we need to be patient with ourselves and others as we learn to communicate more effectively.

Furthermore, the Bible itself offers countless examples of effective communication. Consider the parables of Jesus:

His stories were carefully crafted to reach his audience, communicating complex truths in simple, relatable ways. He always met people where they were, adapting his communication style to their understanding. Similarly, we need to adapt our communication style to our family members, considering their personalities and understanding their unique needs.

Ultimately, non-violent communication is a spiritual practice. It requires humility, empathy, and a willingness to put the needs of others ahead of our own, reflecting the selflessness of Christ. By embracing NVC, we move towards a more loving, fulfilling, and Christ-centered family life, where disagreements are opportunities for growth, and communication becomes a bridge to deeper understanding and unity.

The practice mirrors God's own patient and forgiving nature, transforming conflict into an opportunity for grace and healing. The goal is to transform our families into reflections of God's own loving community, where each member feels valued, respected, and deeply understood. Remember, it is a continuous process; a journey of growth, fueled by faith and commitment, leading towards a more harmonious and joyful family life, mirroring the peace and love found in God's kingdom.

The more we practice these principles, the more readily they will become second nature. We will find ourselves responding to conflicts with empathy and understanding, fostering an environment of love and respect that strengthens our bonds and brings us closer to one another and, importantly, to God.

## *Chapter 3: Commitment: The Glue that Holds Families Together*

*-Unwavering Commitment in the Face of Challenge*

*-The Power of Shared Goals and Dreams*

*-Prioritizing Family Time Making Time for Connect*

*-Celebrating Milestones and Achievements*

*-Commitment as an Act of Worship*

## Unwavering Commitment in the Face of Challenges

Commitment, that unwavering dedication, forms the bedrock of any thriving family. It's the invisible glue that holds together the laughter, the tears, the triumphs, and the trials. It's the quiet strength that allows a family to weather the storms and emerge stronger on the other side. Without commitment, the bonds that unite a family fray, leaving individuals feeling adrift and disconnected. The Bible offers countless examples of unwavering commitment, illustrating its vital role in God's plan for families.

Consider the steadfastness of Abraham, who obeyed God's call despite the uncertainties ahead, a commitment that blessed generations to come. Or Ruth, who chose loyalty to Naomi, showcasing unwavering commitment in the face of immense hardship, a commitment that eventually led to blessings beyond her wildest dreams. These biblical narratives aren't simply historical accounts; they're powerful illustrations of the enduring strength that unwavering commitment provides.

In the context of modern family life, maintaining this commitment often requires intentional effort. The pressures of daily life – work demands, financial strains, personal conflicts – can easily erode the foundation of commitment. Yet, it's during these challenging times that commitment shines brightest. It's the choice to persevere, to remain steadfast in your vows, to prioritize your family's well-being even when it's difficult. It's a conscious decision to choose love over resentment, forgiveness over bitterness, unity over division.

One crucial aspect of maintaining commitment is cultivating a shared vision for your family's future. This shared vision isn't simply a list of goals; it's a deeply held belief system that guides your actions and decisions. It's the shared understanding of your family values, the principles that you strive to live by, and the aspirations you hold for your children and your relationship. For example, a family might share a commitment to faith, education, and service to the community. This shared vision provides a north star, guiding them through the inevitable storms and challenges that life throws their way. When difficulties arise, the family can always return to their shared vision, reminding themselves of the common ground that binds them together. They can draw strength from their shared commitment to their values and goals, providing the resilience to overcome obstacles.

Another vital component is the intentional cultivation of family time. In our busy, technology-driven world, it's easy to allow work, social media, and individual pursuits to consume our time, leaving little space for meaningful family interactions. However, dedicated family time isn't simply about being physically together; it's about creating space for genuine connection and interaction. It's about putting away distractions, engaging in conversations, and sharing experiences. This might involve regular family dinners, game nights, weekend outings, or even simply quiet moments of shared reading or conversation. The key is to create consistent, dedicated time for family bonding, fostering strong emotional bonds and shared memories. Regular family prayer time, reading scriptures together, and discussing faith-related topics can significantly strengthen family unity and deepen commitment.

Furthermore, commitment involves celebrating milestones and achievements – both big and small. Marking birthdays, anniversaries, graduations, and other significant occasions creates shared memories and strengthens the emotional bonds within a family. These celebrations, whether they are elaborate affairs or quiet family gatherings, serve as opportunities to express appreciation, acknowledge achievements, and reaffirm your commitment to one another. Even small gestures of love and affection – a kind word, a helping hand, a spontaneous act of service – strengthen your commitment and express your love to each other.

Consider the example of a family navigating a serious illness. The unwavering commitment displayed during this time, the sacrifices made, the shared burden carried – these actions solidify their family bonds, revealing the profound depth of their mutual commitment.

The commitment to persevere through hardship, to offer support and encouragement, to hold onto hope – this strengthens not just their family, but also their faith. The strength they draw from their shared commitment to each other and their faith provides the resilience to overcome the challenge and emerge even stronger.

The commitment necessary for a thriving family extends beyond the immediate family unit. It often involves extending that commitment to extended family, friends, and community. Supporting elderly parents, caring for siblings in need, or volunteering in the community all reflect the outward expression of a committed heart. This outward focus helps shift the emphasis away from personal concerns, fostering a deeper appreciation for the blessings in their own family life. This outward-focused commitment further strengthens the family's bond by cultivating gratitude, humility, and empathy.

Commitment is not a passive state; it's an active, ongoing process that requires continuous effort and intentionality. It's about making choices, daily and consistently, that reaffirm your dedication to your family. It's about prioritizing their well-being over personal desires, and about forgiving offenses and moving forward with compassion and understanding. It's about choosing love, even when it's difficult.

Moreover, understanding commitment as an act of worship to God significantly deepens its meaning and impact.

Commitment to family is not just a human endeavor; it's a reflection of our commitment to God and His plan for our lives. By viewing our commitment to family through a spiritual lens, we can understand it as a sacred calling, a way to honor God and reflect His love in our actions and interactions. This perspective strengthens our commitment by providing a deeper purpose and motivation.

It allows us to view challenges not as obstacles but as opportunities for spiritual growth and a deeper connection with God and our families.

Commitment, then, is not merely a feeling; it's a conscious decision, a daily practice, and an act of faith. It's the steadfast resolve that binds a family together through both joy and sorrow, success and failure, and growth and change. It's the unwavering dedication that allows a family to not just survive, but to truly thrive. It's the strength that allows them to face life's inevitable storms and emerge not only unscathed but stronger and more united than before.

It is, in essence, the very essence of a family's enduring strength, a testament to love, resilience, and the enduring power of faith. It's a journey of continuous growth and refinement, a testament to the commitment made, and the commitment that continues to be nurtured, day by day, year by year. This enduring commitment is the true glue that holds families together, reflecting God's own unwavering commitment to us, and a reflection of the love and grace He so freely bestows. Nurturing this commitment is not just a responsibility; it's a privilege, a pathway to experiencing the profound blessings of a truly unified and loving family.

## The Power of Shared Goals and Dreams

The blend of family life is richly woven with individual threads of dreams and aspirations. Each member contributes their unique colors and textures, creating a masterpiece that reflects the collective spirit of the family unit. But what happens when these individual threads pull in different directions, creating tension and fraying the fabric of the family? The answer lies in the power of shared goals and dreams—a unifying force that binds individual ambitions into a cohesive and purposeful whole. It's about weaving these individual threads together, not into a bland uniformity, but into a vibrant and richly textured design, reflecting the unique beauty of each member while simultaneously creating something greater than the sum of its parts. This shared vision isn't about sacrificing individual passions; rather, it's about finding a harmonious way for these passions to contribute to the family's overall narrative.

Consider the parable of the builders in **Matthew 7:24-27** . Two men build houses; one on the rock, the other on sand. The storms of life inevitably come, but the house built on the solid foundation of faith and shared purpose stands firm. The family that builds its foundation on shared goals, dreams, and a commitment to God's will is similarly resilient. They face challenges together, supporting and encouraging one another, because they are bound by a shared purpose—a vision that transcends individual ambitions. This shared vision doesn't eliminate personal growth; instead, it provides a framework within which individual aspirations can flourish. It's about a common destination, a shared journey, where individual talents and skills contribute to a collective purpose. The family becomes a team, working together to achieve what none could achieve alone.

This shared vision isn't simply about achieving materialistic goals, but something far more profound. It's about cultivating a deep sense of belonging, purpose, and mutual support. It's about creating a family culture where individual dreams are not only tolerated but celebrated and actively supported. It involves open communication where family members feel safe to share their hopes, fears, and ambitions. It means engaging in honest conversations about what matters most—both individually and collectively—and finding ways to integrate those values into a shared family vision. This shared vision is not a static entity; it's an evolving narrative, shaped and reshaped by the changing dynamics of family life. It's a living document, continually refined and adapted as individual needs and circumstances evolve.

For example, consider the Johnson family. Mr. Johnson, a hardworking carpenter, dreamed of owning his own workshop. Mrs.Johnson, a gifted artist, aspired to teach art classes in the community. Their teenage daughter, Sarah, yearned to travel the world, while their younger son, David, showed a remarkable aptitude for music. Initially, their individual aspirations seemed disparate, even conflicting, potentially creating friction and division. However, through open communication and prayer, they discovered a shared vision: to create a family life filled with creativity, service, and shared experiences. Mr. Johnson's workshop became a family project, where Sarah helped with the carpentry and David played music while they worked. Mrs. Johnson's art classes became a family affair, with the children assisting in preparing materials and learning new techniques.

As they worked towards their individual dreams, they found synergy and mutual support; their individual aspirations were integrated into their shared family mission, creating a stronger bond and deeper sense of belonging. The family's shared vision wasn't just a collection of individual ambitions; it became the foundation upon which their relationships thrived.

The power of shared goals and dreams extends far beyond the immediate family. It touches the wider community, fostering a sense of responsibility and social contribution. Families that have a shared commitment to helping others, for instance, often find their bonds strengthened through shared service. Volunteering as a family, engaging in community projects, or simply supporting each other in acts of kindness to neighbours and friends cultivates a sense of unity, fosters empathy, and instills a strong moral compass in children.

This outward-focused approach creates a virtuous cycle; it strengthens the family unit while making a positive impact on the wider community. This outward focus reinforces the internal unity, creating a shared identity that transcends mere biological relationships.

The family is not just a collection of individuals under one roof; it becomes a force for good, impacting the lives of others. Moreover, the pursuit of shared goals and dreams provides a framework for navigating life's inevitable challenges. When faced with adversity, families with a shared vision are better equipped to cope with difficulties. They have a common purpose to hold onto, a shared sense of resilience, and the strength that comes from working together through difficult times. This shared sense of purpose provides a sense of stability during tumultuous times; it's an anchor that keeps them grounded and focused, preventing them from being swept away by the storms of life.

It's the foundation upon which they can rebuild and emerge stronger from difficult situations, their bond fortified by the shared experience of facing adversity together. This shared struggle fosters a deeper understanding and appreciation for one another, creating a resilience that's far greater than the sum of its parts. Consider the biblical example of Joseph and his brothers. Though initially marked by betrayal and conflict, their relationship ultimately transformed into a story of forgiveness, reconciliation, and unwavering commitment to their shared family destiny.

Despite the years of separation and hardship, the shared familial bond ultimately prevailed, leading to a profound reconciliation and a shared future that blessed generations to come. Their story serves as a powerful reminder of the enduring power of family—even in the face of overwhelming adversity.

It demonstrates that shared goals and dreams, even amidst conflict and hardship, can ultimately forge stronger bonds and deeper connections within the family unit. The journey of reconciliation is an arduous one, but it highlights the profound strength that comes from shared commitment, even when that commitment requires forgiveness, empathy, and unwavering faith.

The cultivation of shared goals and dreams requires consistent effort and intentional nurturing. It's not a passive process; it requires active participation from each family member, fostering a sense of ownership and responsibility. Regular family meetings, for instance, can provide a forum for open communication, sharing aspirations, and collaboratively developing a shared family vision. Family rituals and traditions further solidify these bonds, creating shared memories and a sense of belonging. These rituals don't have to be elaborate; it's about creating shared experiences that build a sense of unity and connection, forming the strong ties that help families weather the storms of life. Consistent participation in these rituals further solidifies these bonds and deepens the family's shared identity. These shared moments become pillars in the overall family narrative.

The integration of faith into the family's shared vision adds another layer of depth and purpose. A family grounded in their faith will approach their shared goals and dreams with a spirit of humility, service, and gratitude. They will recognize that their achievements are not solely the result of their own efforts but also a blessing from God. This perspective instills a sense of perspective, keeping their goals aligned with their values and preventing them from being consumed by materialistic pursuits. This perspective also promotes gratitude and appreciation for the blessings in their lives, creating a family culture of thankfulness and contentment. This integration of faith fosters a deeper sense of purpose, guiding their shared journey and providing strength during challenging times.

In conclusion, the power of shared goals and dreams lies in its ability to unify a family, creating a sense of purpose, belonging, and resilience. It's not about erasing individual aspirations; rather, it's about finding a harmonious way to weave them together, creating a beautiful and strong tapestry that reflects the unique beauty and strength of each member while simultaneously achieving something greater than the sum of its parts. It is a journey of continuous growth and refinement, a testament to the commitment made and the commitment that continues to be nurtured, day by day, year by year.

Building a family around shared goals and dreams isn't just about achieving specific objectives; it's about creating a life filled with love, joy, and a shared sense of purpose, grounded in faith and strengthened by unwavering commitment. This, truly, is the glue that holds families together and allows them to not only survive but thrive, reflecting God's own unwavering commitment to us and a reflection of the love and grace He so freely bestows.

## *Prioritizing Family Time Making Time for Connection*

The previous chapter emphasized the foundational importance of shared goals and dreams in building a strong family unit. But even the most ambitious family vision will crumble without the crucial ingredient of dedicated time spent together. This isn't merely about quantity—it's about quality, about creating a space where hearts connect, conversations flow freely, and the bonds of love are strengthened. In today's fast-paced world, filled with competing demands and distractions, intentionally carving out this time is an act of profound commitment, a testament to the value we place on our family relationships. It is a deliberate act of worship, mirroring God's own unwavering commitment to us, reflected in the consistent, steadfast presence of His love.

Think of it like this: a gardener wouldn't expect a flourishing garden without regular tending. Weeding, watering, and nurturing are essential to growth. Similarly, family relationships require intentional cultivation. We must actively cultivate connection, fostering a climate of love, understanding, and shared experiences.This involves setting aside specific times for family activities, creating rituals that become cherished traditions, and cultivating an environment where open communication thrives.

The challenge, of course, lies in the practical application. Many families grapple with busy schedules, demanding careers, and numerous responsibilities.

How then, can we effectively prioritize family time in the midst of a life that often feels overwhelmingly busy? The answer lies not in magic solutions but in a thoughtful, strategic approach. It begins with a honest assessment of our current time allocation. Where are our priorities truly located? Are we spending our precious time in ways that reflect our commitment to our families, or are we allowing other commitments to overshadow what truly matters?

Consider the parable of the talents in **Matthew 25** . The master entrusts his servants with varying amounts of talents, expecting them to utilize them wisely. Similarly, God entrusts us with our time, a precious resource that should be used to build His Kingdom, starting within our own homes. Neglecting our families, neglecting that time for connection, is a form of neglecting the stewardship God has given us.

One practical strategy is to create a family calendar, a visual representation of everyone's schedules. This allows for a collaborative approach to planning family time. Each member can contribute their ideas and preferences, fostering a sense of ownership and shared responsibility. This isn't about dictating schedules; it's about working together to create a harmonious rhythm that accommodates everyone's needs while prioritizing family connection. Family meetings, even short ones, can be invaluable for this process. These aren't about lectures, but rather opportunities for open dialogue, brainstorming ideas, and ensuring everyone feels heard and valued.

Prioritizing family time isn't just about creating moments; it's about creating memories. These memories become the mortar that binds the family unit, providing a shared narrative that strengthens bonds and creates lasting connections. This doesn't necessitate grand gestures or extravagant vacations. It can be as simple as a weekly family game night, a regular Sunday dinner, or a shared bedtime story. The key is consistency and intentionality.

Think back to your own childhood. What are the memories that stand out most vividly? Are they related to material possessions, or are they moments of shared laughter, connection, and unconditional love? The enduring power of these memories underscores the importance of prioritizing quality time over quantity. It's important to recognize that "quality time" isn't about the absence of distractions. It's about presence. It's about being fully engaged with each other, listening attentively, and demonstrating genuine interest in one another's lives.

Even during busy evenings, incorporating intentional connection points can make a significant difference. While dinner is being prepared, perhaps engage in a meaningful conversation or listen to your children's accounts of their day. Consider setting aside time for a family walk, or turning off all electronics during dinner, ensuring everyone's focus is on connection, not just sustenance. Consider having a tech-free hour before bed as a consistent practice. This fosters a space for intimate conversations and bonding, allowing your family to wind down and be present together. Another significant element is creating family rituals and traditions.

These become anchors in the midst of life's chaos, providing stability and a shared sense of identity. Perhaps it's a yearly camping trip, a monthly movie night, or a weekly tradition of baking cookies together. The specific rituals are less important than the act of creating them and nurturing them over time. These traditions reinforce family bonds and create lasting memories that will be cherished for years to come.

For families with multiple children, prioritizing individual time is equally crucial. This might involve setting aside specific times for one-on-one conversations or activities with each child. This shows that each child is valued and loved individually, strengthening the individual child-parent bond, while also demonstrating the importance of prioritizing each family member within the larger context of the family unit. This is an act of individualized love and commitment.

Remember, creating time for family also includes the necessity of rest and renewal. We cannot pour from an empty cup. Parents who are stressed, burnt out, and lacking in self-care, are less capable of giving their best to their families. Prioritizing individual rest isn't selfish; it's essential. Taking time for personal prayer, reflection, or engaging in hobbies that bring joy and renewal, allows individuals to return to their family relationships refreshed and energized. This is not just for parents.

Teaching children the value of rest, and creating opportunities for personal reflection within the family unit is a vital aspect of creating a healthy and well-balanced family dynamic. It teaches self-care and self-compassion, which are crucial to personal well-being and strengthening the foundation of family relationships. A family that thrives on prioritizing rest for its members, prioritizes wholeness and resilience.

In conclusion, prioritizing family time is a continuous journey, a commitment that requires consistent effort, intentionality, and flexibility. It's not about perfection; it's about progress. Even small acts of connection, however seemingly insignificant, contribute to the overall tapestry of family life. It's about creating a safe haven, a place where each member feels loved, accepted, and cherished. It is a commitment that reflects the very essence of God's love for us – a love that is consistent, unwavering, and full of grace.

By mirroring that love within our own families, we are building a testament to God's grace, a legacy that will extend far beyond our own lifetimes. This commitment, this dedication to connection, is the very heart of a thriving, loving family, strengthened by faith and sustained by the unwavering grace of God.

## Celebrating Milestones and Achievements

The previous chapter focused on the vital role of dedicated family time in nurturing strong bonds. But a truly thriving family isn't just built on shared moments; it's also nourished by the shared experiences of celebrating life's milestones, both big and small. These celebrations aren't mere formalities; they're powerful rituals that weave the threads of joy, gratitude, and unity into the fabric of family life, reflecting the abundant blessings God bestows upon us. Celebrating achievements, whether a child's first step or a parent's career milestone, is an act of acknowledging God's hand in our lives, a recognition of His provision and grace.

Think of it as a family's own unique symphony, each accomplishment a note played in harmony, creating a beautiful melody of shared experiences and collective joy. These celebratory moments aren't just about the event itself; they're about creating lasting memories, strengthening emotional connections, and solidifying the sense of belonging that is so crucial for a healthy family unit. It's about acknowledging the individual journeys of each family member within the broader context of the family's shared narrative.

Consider the simple act of celebrating a child's first day of school. It might seem like a small event, a fleeting moment in the grand scheme of things. Yet, for the child, it's a significant milestone, a step towards independence and growth. For parents, it's a mixture of pride, nostalgia, and perhaps a touch of bittersweet emotion as they watch their little one embark on this new adventure. A family celebration – a small breakfast, a special photograph, a heartfelt conversation – transforms this ordinary event into an extraordinary memory, a shared experience that binds them together.

The same principle applies to larger milestones. Graduations, weddings, anniversaries – these are pivotal moments that call for more elaborate celebrations, but the essence remains the same: the creation of shared memories, the affirmation of love and support, the strengthening of family bonds. The specific nature of the celebration is less important than the intention behind it – the desire to honor the achievement and to share in the joy of the occasion. Remember, it's the quality of the time spent together, the genuine expression of love and appreciation, that truly matters.

The Bible itself is filled with examples of celebrating milestones. Consider the Passover, a celebration commemorating the Israelites' liberation from slavery in Egypt. This annual observance serves as a powerful reminder of God's faithfulness and His deliverance, strengthening their identity as a people chosen by God. Similarly, the Feast of Tabernacles, celebrating the harvest and God's provision, fostered a sense of community and gratitude. These events weren't simply historical re-enactments; they were vibrant expressions of faith, family, and communal identity, reinforcing their commitment to God and to one another.

In modern family life, the ways we celebrate milestones are as diverse as the families themselves. Some families might opt for large gatherings with extended family and friends, complete with elaborate meals, speeches, and gifts. Others may prefer smaller, more intimate celebrations, focusing on quality time together and meaningful gestures. The important thing is that the celebration genuinely reflects the family's values and traditions, creating a unique tapestry of shared experiences that become part of their collective story.

Think about the family that gathers every year for a summer picnic in a favourite park. It's not just about the food; it's about the tradition, the shared laughter, the opportunity to connect amidst the beauty of nature. Or consider the family that starts a new tradition of watching a favorite movie together every Friday night, creating a consistent space for connection and shared enjoyment.

Even something as simple as a weekly family dinner, where everyone gathers around the table to share stories and connect, can become a powerful ritual that strengthens family bonds. Let's consider a family celebrating a child's graduation from college. The celebration might involve a formal dinner, a heartfelt speech from a family member, or perhaps a slideshow of photos chronicling the child's journey through school. The celebration isn't just about acknowledging the academic achievement; it's about acknowledging the years of hard work, dedication, and perseverance. It's about celebrating the child's growth as an individual, and reaffirming the family's unwavering love and support.

In another scenario, we could look at a family celebrating a parent's retirement. The celebration might involve a surprise party with friends and family, a trip to a dream destination, or simply a quiet evening spent reminiscing about past accomplishments and looking forward to the future. The essence of the celebration lies in acknowledging the parent's significant contribution to the family, expressing gratitude for their years of dedication and hard work, and celebrating the new chapter in their life.

The key to successful family celebrations isn't about extravagance or expense. It's about intentionality. It's about creating a space where family members feel seen, heard, and appreciated. It's about taking the time to express gratitude for one another, for the shared journey, and for God's blessings. These celebrations should be a reflection of the family's commitment to one another and their shared faith. It's important to remember that celebrations shouldn't be limited to grand occasions. The seemingly mundane aspects of daily life offer countless opportunities to celebrate small victories and show appreciation.

A simple "thank you" for a kind gesture, a spontaneous hug, or a shared laugh – these small acts of affection create a climate of love and appreciation that strengthens family bonds. Celebrating the small wins, the everyday triumphs, keeps the spirit of celebration alive and strengthens family unity on a daily basis. It cultivates a sense of gratitude and reinforces the feeling of being valued and cherished within the family unit.

Perhaps a child finally mastered a difficult piece on the piano. A spontaneous celebratory ice cream sundae, shared amidst words of encouragement and praise, transforms a personal accomplishment into a shared family moment. Maybe a family member successfully navigated a challenging situation. Celebrating their resilience and strength through a heartfelt conversation and an evening of family togetherness can reaffirm their importance within the family and deepen their sense of belonging.

The beauty of celebrating milestones lies in its adaptability. Each family will discover its own unique ways to commemorate events, forging traditions and memories that reflect their individual personalities and values. There's no one-size-fits-all approach. The crucial element is the consistent effort to acknowledge achievements, big or small, and to express gratitude and appreciation for one another.

Ultimately, celebrating milestones and achievements is an act of faith, a recognition of God's grace and provision in our lives. It's a testament to the value we place on our family relationships and our commitment to nurturing them. By making these celebrations a regular part of our family life, we create a legacy of love, unity, and shared joy that will enrich our lives and the lives of future generations. It's a visible demonstration of our faith, reflecting God's own boundless love and celebrating the gifts He has bestowed upon us.

This commitment to celebrating, even in the midst of challenges, is a testament to our faith and our trust in His unwavering plan for our families. Through these celebrations, we build a strong foundation of love, gratitude, and unity, creating a family that truly reflects the grace and love of God.

## Commitment as an Act of Worship

The previous chapter spoke of celebrating life's milestones as a testament to our faith. But the bedrock upon which those celebrations, and indeed the entire structure of a thriving family, rests is unwavering commitment. This isn't merely a matter of sticking it out through thick and thin; it's a conscious, daily act of worship, a reflection of our devotion to God's plan for our lives and the families He has entrusted to us. Think of it as a living sacrifice, offered not on an altar of stone, but on the altar of our daily lives, a constant offering of our will to His.

Consider the parable of the talents in **Matthew 25** . The master entrusts his servants with varying amounts of wealth, and the rewards are directly correlated to the level of commitment shown in managing those talents. The servant who buried his talent, essentially choosing inaction and a lack of commitment, faced severe consequences. Similarly, in our family lives, a lack of commitment, a failure to invest our time, energy, and love, can lead to barrenness and disappointment.

But when we approach family life with a committed heart, actively engaging in nurturing, supporting, and loving our spouses and children, we are not simply fulfilling a duty, but fulfilling a divine calling. We are mirroring God's own relentless commitment to us, His unwavering love despite our flaws and failures.

This commitment, however, isn't a cold, calculating adherence to a checklist of responsibilities. It's an outpouring of love, fueled by faith and strengthened by prayer. It's the willingness to sacrifice personal desires for the greater good of the family unit, recognizing that true fulfillment lies not in individual ambition, but in shared purpose and mutual support.

This may involve sacrificing career advancements for family needs, foregoing personal hobbies to attend a child's school event, or putting aside personal grievances to foster unity within the home.

These acts of selflessness, these small but significant sacrifices, are powerful expressions of our commitment, a testament to the depth of our faith and our understanding of God's priorities. The **book of Ephesians** provides a powerful model for committed family life. Paul's instruction to wives to submit to their husbands, and husbands to love their wives as Christ loved the church, isn't a call to subservience, but a call to selfless love and mutual respect. It's a call to a partnership built on shared faith and a commitment to serving one another.

When we view our family relationships through the lens of this sacrificial love, commitment becomes less of a burden and more of a privilege. It becomes an opportunity to reflect Christ's own unwavering love for His people, an opportunity to demonstrate the transformative power of grace.

Furthermore, commitment extends beyond the immediate family unit. It encompasses our commitment to our extended family, our church community, and our wider society. Supporting aging parents, mentoring younger generations, serving the needs of others– these are all expressions of our commitment to living out God's love in the world. They are tangible manifestations of our faith, demonstrating the depth of our devotion and our understanding that we are all interconnected members of God's family.

I recall a couple I counseled, Sarah and David. Their marriage was teetering on the brink of collapse. Years of unresolved conflict, unmet expectations, and a general lack of communication had eroded the foundation of their relationship. Yet, amidst the turmoil, there was a flicker of faith, a shared desire to salvage their marriage, a commitment, however fragile, to work towards reconciliation. It was a commitment born not of human strength, but of a shared prayer, a plea for divine intervention.

The journey was arduous, filled with tears, admissions of fault, and the painstaking work of rebuilding trust. It required a willingness to compromise, to forgive, and to constantly seek God's guidance. But through it all, their commitment remained steadfast. They attended counseling sessions, diligently worked through their issues, and, most importantly, prayed together consistently. They saw their commitment as an act of worship, a testament to their faith in God's power to heal and restore. And God did just that. Today, Sarah and David's marriage is a testament to the transformative power of committed faith, a beacon of hope for those struggling to maintain their own family bonds. Their story isn't an exception, but a reminder of the profound impact of committed faith and unwavering devotion in the context of family life.

We often confuse commitment with simply enduring hardship. It's easy to view commitment as grim perseverance through difficulties.While perseverance is certainly a component, commitment is far richer and more rewarding. It's an active participation in the growth and flourishing of our families, a conscious choice to invest our time, energy, and love in nurturing our relationships. It's about choosing faith over fear, hope over despair, and love over apathy. It is about choosing to constantly communicate openly, honestly, and respectfully, not just when things are easy. It requires a commitment to consistent prayer, seeking God's wisdom and strength to navigate the inevitable challenges of family life.

Think of the shepherd in **Psalm 23** . His unwavering commitment to his flock, guiding them through green pastures and beside still waters, is a beautiful metaphor for God's commitment to us, and our commitment to our families. Just as the shepherd protects and provides for his sheep, we too are called to protect and provide for our loved ones, to guide them, to nurture them, and to lead them towards a deeper relationship with God. This is not a task we undertake alone; it is a journey we walk together, hand in hand, with God as our guide and our strength. This is commitment as an act of worship: a continual, conscious, and deeply personal dedication to the divine blueprint for family life. Commitment isn't about perfection; it's about perseverance. It's about recognizing that families are messy, imperfect, and often frustrating. Yet, it is within these imperfections that God's grace shines most brightly. It is in our failures and our struggles that we learn the true meaning of commitment, the value of forgiveness, and the transformative power of unwavering faith.

The commitment to our families isn't just a moral imperative; it's a spiritual practice. It's a way of offering ourselves, our time, our energy, and our love, as a living sacrifice to God. It's a way of honoring His plan for our lives, and for the families He has blessed us with. And in that act of worship, in that unwavering commitment, we discover not only a stronger family, but a deeper, richer relationship with God Himself. The blessings that flow from this kind of commitment are immeasurable, enriching not only our families but also our own souls.

This is the legacy we build, a legacy not of material wealth, but of faith, love, and unwavering commitment – a testament to the power of God's grace working in and through our lives. And it's a legacy that continues to bless generations to come. This is the true heart of commitment as an act of worship.

## Chapter 4: Compromise: The Art of Mutual Respect

-Learning to Yield Embracing Mutual Respect

-Negotiation Skills for Family Harmony

-The Role of Empathy in Compromise

-Compromise as an Expression of Love

-Avoiding Power Struggles Through Compromise

## Learning to Yield Embracing Mutual Respect

Compromise isn't about losing; it's about winning together. It's a fundamental principle, woven into the very fabric of healthy relationships, mirroring the intricate dance of giving and receiving that defines true love. In the tapestry of family life, compromise acts as the strong thread that binds individual strands into a beautiful, cohesive whole. Without it, the threads fray, the pattern unravels, and the beauty of the fabric is lost.

The Bible, a rich source of wisdom for navigating life's complexities, offers numerous examples of compromise, illustrating its profound significance in building strong and enduring relationships. Consider the story of Abraham and Lot. Facing a disagreement over pastureland, Abraham, the elder and arguably more powerful, willingly yields, offering Lot the first choice. This act of selflessness prevents conflict and exemplifies a willingness to prioritize harmony over personal gain. It teaches us that true strength lies not in dominance, but in humility and the understanding that sometimes, yielding is a powerful act of love.

Think also of Joseph, whose remarkable story of forgiveness and reconciliation stands as a powerful testament to the transformative power of compromise. Betrayed and sold into slavery by his own brothers, Joseph could have easily succumbed to bitterness and vengeance. Instead, he chooses mercy, forgiveness, and reconciliation. His act of yielding, of letting go of past hurts, ultimately leads to the salvation of his family and a profound restoration of their relationships. This underscores a crucial element of compromise: it requires letting go of resentment, pride, and the need to always be "right." In our modern lives, the need for compromise extends beyond grand narratives and biblical parables. It manifests in the daily choices we make within our families – from deciding on dinner menus to navigating the complexities of parenting.

A parent might compromise on a child's bedtime request, understanding the child's need for a little extra time, while still maintaining a consistent routine. A couple might compromise on vacation plans, balancing individual preferences to create a mutually satisfying experience. These seemingly small acts of compromise build trust, respect, and a sense of shared ownership in the family dynamic. They signal to each other and to the children, that everyone's voice matters, and everyone's needs are considered.

The art of yielding, however, doesn't mean surrendering one's values or beliefs. True compromise involves finding common ground, a space where individual needs and desires can coexist harmoniously. It's about finding creative solutions that acknowledge and respect the perspectives of all involved. This might mean modifying individual plans to accommodate shared goals, or finding alternative solutions that address the concerns of everyone involved. It is about negotiation, not capitulation.

Learning to yield requires a willingness to listen, truly listen, to understand the perspectives of others.

This involves putting aside our own biases and preconceived notions, and actively seeking to understand the reasoning behind another person's viewpoint. It demands empathy, the ability to step into someone else's shoes and see the world from their perspective. Only through true understanding can we find solutions that are mutually beneficial.

Effective communication is the cornerstone of successful compromise. Open and honest dialogue, free from judgment and criticism, creates an environment where differences can be aired without fear of retribution. This involves expressing our own needs and wants clearly and respectfully, while actively listening to the responses of others. It means using "I" statements to convey our feelings without blaming or accusing, and actively seeking clarification to ensure understanding. It involves being willing to explain our reasoning, to demonstrate our willingness to meet each other halfway.

The process of compromise is often a negotiation, a dance of give-and-take. It requires flexibility and a willingness to adjust one's position to reach a mutually agreeable outcome. Sometimes, this may involve concessions; other times, it may involve creative problem-solving. The key is to maintain a collaborative spirit, where all parties work together towards a common goal. The goal isn't necessarily to satisfy everyone completely, but to create a solution that works for everyone, even if it's not ideal for any single person.

Moreover, compromise should never be seen as a sign of weakness.Instead, it demonstrates strength of character, a willingness to prioritize relationships over individual desires. It's an act of love, a testament to the value placed on maintaining harmony and unity within the family. It shows a maturity that comes from understanding that the well-being of the entire unit outweighs any personal preference.

There are times when compromise feels impossible, when the differences seem insurmountable. But even in these challenging moments, faith plays a crucial role. Prayer can provide the guidance and strength needed to navigate difficult conversations and find creative solutions. Seeking divine wisdom can illuminate paths that might not be readily apparent. Trusting in God's plan can provide the peace and confidence necessary to approach these situations with humility and a willingness to yield.

The principle of compromise is not merely a pragmatic approach to conflict resolution; it's a spiritual practice that reflects the very essence of Christ's teachings. His willingness to lay down his life for humanity, to sacrifice his own desires for the well-being of others, stands as the ultimate example of compromise and selfless love. His life serves as a constant reminder that true fulfillment comes not from self-preservation, but from self-giving. By embracing compromise in our relationships, we are reflecting the love and compassion of Christ, strengthening the bonds that unite our families and fostering a deeper sense of community. Consider the parable of the talents. The master entrusts his servants with different amounts of talent, recognizing their individual capabilities and responsibilities. While expectations vary, the master rewards faithfulness and diligence. This parable speaks to the importance of individual contributions while maintaining a unified purpose. Similarly, within a family, each member has unique skills, talents, and contributions to offer. Compromise allows for these differences to be acknowledged and celebrated, creating a synergy that strengthens the whole.

In the practical application of compromise, it's vital to remember that it is a two-way street. It requires both parties to be willing to participate, to negotiate, and to find common ground. It is not about one party consistently giving in or always compromising their needs. It's about a balance, a mutual understanding of give-and-take. This balance ensures fairness and prevents resentment, maintaining the healthy dynamic of a strong relationship. A consistently one-sided compromise will eventually crumble under the weight of unmet needs and resentment. It's about understanding that a true compromise is beneficial for everyone involved. Furthermore, effective compromise requires a willingness to forgive.

Past hurts and misunderstandings can hinder the ability to compromise. Holding onto past grievances creates barriers that prevent open communication and trust. Forgiveness, therefore, is an essential ingredient for successful compromise. It's about letting go of anger, resentment, and the desire to seek retribution. It's about choosing to move forward and creating a more positive future together.

This forgiveness is not necessarily forgetting, but it's about choosing to release the pain and focus on building a stronger relationship going forward. In essence, forgiveness paves the way for a harmonious and successful compromise.

In conclusion, compromise is not a weakness but a strength, a testament to the love and respect that bind families together. It's a journey of mutual understanding, a dance of give-and-take, a testament to the willingness to put the needs of the whole above individual preferences. By embracing the art of yielding and finding common ground, we build stronger, more resilient relationships, reflecting the love and compassion of Christ and creating a harmonious home where all can thrive.

It's a path that leads to greater peace, deeper understanding, and more fulfilling relationships. It's a spiritual practice that nurtures the soul and strengthens the bonds of family life, creating a collage of love, unity, and lasting joy. And that, ultimately, is what truly matters.

## Negotiation Skills for Family Harmony

Building upon the foundation of compromise as a cornerstone of family harmony, we now delve into the practical application of negotiation skills. This isn't about manipulation or forcing a solution, but about fostering an environment where every voice is heard, respected, and valued. Think of it as a collaborative effort, a team working towards a common goal – a peaceful, loving home.

The Bible consistently emphasizes the importance of unity and understanding within the family unit, echoing the image of the body of Christ, where each member plays a vital role. Just as different parts of the body work together harmoniously, so too should the members of a family. Effective communication is the bedrock of successful negotiation.

This isn't simply about talking; it's about truly listening, understanding the perspectives of each family member, and validating their feelings. Often, conflicts arise not because of irreconcilable differences, but because of a lack of understanding. One might recall the parable of the talents in **Matthew 25:14-30** , where the master commends the servants who diligently used their talents, highlighting the importance of understanding individual strengths and perspectives. In a family setting, this means actively seeking to understand why each member feels a certain way, rather than dismissing their feelings. Empathetic listening, where you put yourself in their shoes and try to comprehend their viewpoint, is crucial.

This principle of active listening is further underscored in **Proverbs 18:13: "He who answers before he listens— that is his folly and his shame."** Impulsive responses often escalate conflicts. Instead, practice patience. Give each family member ample time to express their thoughts and feelings without interruption. Creating a safe space where everyone feels comfortable sharing their concerns is paramount. Consider implementing family meetings where everyone has a designated time to speak, ensuring that each voice is heard without being overshadowed. Remember, the goal isn't to win an argument but to find a solution that works for everyone.

Once everyone has had a chance to express their viewpoints, the next step is to identify the core issue at hand. Often, conflicts are fueled by underlying assumptions and unmet needs. Let's say, for example, a family is arguing over screen time. The surface issue might be the amount of time spent on devices, but the underlying issue could be a feeling of neglect, a desire for connection, or a struggle with self-discipline. By identifying the root cause, you can address the actual problem, rather than simply treating the symptoms. This process requires careful reflection and thoughtful questioning. Ask yourselves: What are the underlying needs and desires fueling this conflict? What fears and insecurities are at play?

Once the core issue is identified, the family can begin to brainstorm solutions together. This is where creativity and flexibility come into play. Instead of approaching negotiations as a win-lose scenario, aim for a win-win solution – an outcome where everyone feels heard and their needs are, at least partially, met. This requires a willingness to compromise and find common ground. Think of it as a collaborative puzzle where each family member contributes a piece to create a complete and satisfying picture. This approach mirrors the collaborative nature of God's kingdom, where unity and cooperation are central themes.

For instance, let's consider a family struggling to manage household chores. Instead of imposing a rigid chore chart, the family could engage in a collaborative discussion, considering each member's strengths, preferences, and availability. One family member might be particularly adept at cooking, while another excels at cleaning. By assigning chores based on individual talents and preferences, the family can ensure a more equitable and efficient distribution of work, promoting a sense of shared responsibility and accomplishment.

Furthermore, effective negotiation involves understanding the concept of "give and take." It's rarely possible to have everything you want. Compromise necessitates relinquishing some individual desires for the benefit of the whole family. This is not a sign of weakness but a demonstration of love and respect for others. This mirrors Christ's own example of self-sacrifice and humility, as highlighted in **Philippians 2:3-11** .

By putting the needs of the family ahead of individual preferences, we create an environment of mutual respect and understanding.

Negotiation also requires patience and persistence. Reaching a mutually agreeable solution doesn't always happen overnight. There may be setbacks, disagreements, and even emotional outbursts. It's important to remain calm, patient, and persistent in the pursuit of a peaceful resolution. Consider the parable of the persistent widow in **Luke 18:1-8** . Her unwavering persistence in seeking justice exemplifies the importance of persevering in the face of challenges. Similarly, family negotiations require resilience and a willingness to revisit issues as needed.

Another critical aspect of successful negotiation is the development of empathy and understanding. Try to see the situation from each family member's perspective. What are their motivations? What are their concerns? Actively seeking to understand the other person's feelings and needs can significantly enhance the negotiation process. This understanding is vital for building trust and rapport, creating an environment where open and honest communication can flourish. The Apostle Paul's instruction in **1 Corinthians 13:4-7** highlights the importance of love, patience, and kindness in our interactions with others. These qualities are essential for successful family negotiations.

Finally, don't forget the importance of celebrating successes, no matter how small.

Acknowledging and appreciating the efforts of each family member in reaching a compromise strengthens the bonds of unity and collaboration. This positive reinforcement encourages future cooperation and fosters a sense of shared accomplishment. Celebrate the victories, both big and small, to maintain a positive and encouraging family atmosphere. This reflects the joy and celebration that permeates the teachings of Jesus Christ, emphasizing the importance of rejoicing in the unity and harmony of the family unit.

In conclusion, effective negotiation within a family is not just a skill; it's a spiritual practice. It requires a conscious effort to prioritize love, empathy, understanding, and a willingness to compromise. By applying these skills, families can transform conflicts into opportunities for growth, strengthening their bonds and creating a more harmonious and fulfilling home environment, reflecting the love and unity found in the heart of God.

The journey may have its bumps and detours, but the destination – a family united in love and understanding – is well worth the effort. This approach, deeply rooted in biblical principles, offers a pathway to lasting peace and joy within the family, a testament to the transformative power of faith and understanding. Through consistent effort and a commitment to Christ-like love, families can cultivate a haven of peace and harmony, creating a lasting legacy of love and mutual respect.

## The Role of Empathy in Compromise

Empathy, that capacity to step into another's shoes and truly understand their feelings, is not merely a desirable trait in compromise; it's the very bedrock upon which successful negotiation is built. Without it, compromise becomes a battle of wills, a tug-of-war where resentment festers rather than resolution blossoms. The Bible, filled with parables and teachings on love and understanding, consistently underscores the importance of considering others' perspectives. Consider the parable of the Good Samaritan – a man who showed extraordinary empathy to a stranger in need, demonstrating a love that transcended societal barriers. This selfless act mirrors the kind of empathy needed in family compromises.

Imagine a family facing a decision about their summer vacation. One child dreams of a bustling theme park, filled with rollercoasters and exhilarating rides, while the other longs for the tranquility of a quiet cabin by the lake, surrounded by nature's quiet beauty. Without empathy, this could easily devolve into a screaming match, each child clinging to their own desire. However, with empathy as a guide, the parents can help each child understand the other's perspective.

The parent might ask the theme-park enthusiast, "Can you imagine how your sibling feels about the loud noises and crowds at a theme park? What if we tried to find a compromise that included elements of both?" Similarly, they might ask the lake-lover, "Think about how exciting the theme park would be for your brother or sister. Could we maybe find a place with some quieter activities, or build in some downtime at the lake?"

This approach doesn't diminish the validity of either child's desires; instead, it acknowledges and respects them. It fosters a sense of understanding and shared responsibility, paving the way for a compromise that considers everyone's needs. Perhaps the solution involves a shorter trip to a theme park followed by a few days of relaxation by a lake, incorporating aspects of both preferences. This outcome isn't just a compromise; it's a collaborative creation, a testament to the power of empathy in achieving a mutually satisfying solution.

The principle extends far beyond vacation planning. Consider a scenario where a couple disagrees about household chores. One partner might feel overwhelmed by the demands of work and childcare, leaving them with little energy for additional household tasks. The other partner, perhaps with more free time, might not fully grasp the extent of the first partner's fatigue. Without
empathy, this could lead to accusations and resentment. However, by empathetically listening to each other's concerns, they can arrive at a more balanced distribution of responsibilities. One partner might take on more of a specific chore, while the other adjusts their schedule to share a different task. The key is to understand the underlying reasons behind the disagreement, not just the surface-level conflict. The application of empathy in family life isn't simply a matter of emotional intelligence; it's a spiritual practicerooted in the teachings of Christ. The Bible consistently urges us to love our neighbors as ourselves, to carry one another's burdens, and to treat others with compassion and understanding. These aren't merely suggestions; they're fundamental principles for building strong, healthy relationships. When we approach disagreements with empathy, we're mirroring the love and grace of God, reflecting His willingness to understand our struggles and offer us forgiveness and reconciliation.

Furthermore, empathy helps us to navigate conflict constructively. It enables us to move beyond the blame game and see the situation from a broader perspective. When we truly understand the other person's feelings, we're less likely to react

defensively or to escalate the conflict. Instead, we can engage in a more thoughtful and
respectful dialogue, seeking a solution that meets the needs of everyone involved. This process often requires a willingness to set aside our own immediate desires and prioritize the well-being of the relationship.

In a family dynamic, this might involve a parent empathizing with a teenager's struggles with peer pressure or academic stress. Instead of simply dismissing the teen's concerns, the parent can actively listen, validate their feelings, and offer support and guidance.

This empathetic approach can build trust and strengthen the parent-child bond, leading to more open communication and a greater willingness to compromise in the future.

However, it's important to note that empathy doesn't mean enabling unhealthy behaviors or ignoring personal boundaries. Empathy is about understanding the *why* behind someone's actions, not condoning the actions themselves. If a child consistently disregards family rules, empathy might help the parent understand the underlying reasons for the child's rebellion, such as feelings of insecurity or unmet needs. However, empathy doesn't negate the need for discipline and setting clear boundaries. Rather, it informs a more compassionate and effective approach to correction.

Moreover, empathy is a reciprocal process. It requires a willingness to both give and receive. In a family context, this means creating a safe and supportive environment where each member feels comfortable expressing their feelings and being heard. This openness and vulnerability are crucial for building trust and fostering empathy among family members. If one member feels consistently disregarded or judged, they're less likely to extend empathy to others.

Therefore, cultivating empathy within the family requires a conscious and ongoing effort. It involves actively listening to others, seeking to understand their perspectives, and responding with compassion and understanding. It's a practice that strengthens relationships, promotes forgiveness, and leads to more effective and meaningful compromises. Just as the body of Christ functions harmoniously through the collaboration of its diverse members, so too can a family flourish through the mutual understanding and empathetic support of its individual members.

The practice of empathy isn't passive; it's actively seeking to understand the emotional landscape of others. It requires asking questions, listening attentively, and reflecting on the information received. It's about seeing the world through someone else's eyes, recognizing their feelings, and validating their experiences, even if we don't necessarily agree with their perspective.

Consider a situation where siblings are fighting over a toy. A simple approach might be to take the toy away. However, an empathetic approach would involve understanding the underlying emotions fueling the conflict. Perhaps one sibling feels overlooked and wants to assert their dominance. Another might feel insecure about their place in the family. Addressing these underlying feelings through empathetic listening can help resolve the conflict more effectively than simply confiscating the toy.

This calls for self-reflection, too. Empathy requires us to understand our own emotional responses and biases, ensuring they don't cloud our judgment. We must be mindful of our own perspectives and how they might influence our understanding of others. This self-awareness is crucial in building a foundation of mutual respect and understanding within the family unit.

Ultimately, the cultivation of empathy within the family is a journey, not a destination. It requires consistent practice, patience, and a willingness to learn and grow. It's a process of continuous self-improvement and strengthening our bonds with one another. Through the practice of empathy, we not only learn to compromise more effectively but also create a deeper, more meaningful connection with our loved ones, reflecting the very essence of God's love and compassion.

This journey, while challenging at times, is richly rewarding, leading to a family unit strengthened by love, understanding, and mutual respect – a testament to the transformative power of empathy. It's a journey worth embracing, one that mirrors the very heart of our faith and strengthens our connections with God and one another.

## Compromise as an Expression of Love

Compromise, far from being a sign of weakness or defeat, is a powerful expression of love, especially within the family unit. It's a conscious decision to prioritize the well-being and happiness of others, a selfless act that mirrors the very essence of Christ's sacrifice for humanity. Think of the countless times Jesus compromised His own comfort and desires for the sake of His followers, His unwavering dedication a testament to the transformative power of love expressed through sacrifice. This same principle applies to our familial relationships. When we willingly compromise, we are not merely resolving a conflict; we are investing in the strength and unity of our family bond.

Consider a family faced with the decision of where to spend their annual vacation. One parent dreams of a relaxing beach getaway, while the other envisions an adventurous mountain hiking trip. Each holds firm to their preference, but the underlying current is a shared desire for a memorable family experience. A compromise, perhaps a week split between a coastal town with hiking trails nearby, would demonstrate love in action. It's a decision where neither parent fully gets their ideal vacation, but both receive the invaluable reward of a shared experience, strengthening their bond and creating lasting memories. This seemingly small act of compromise reflects a profound understanding: that family unity surpasses individual desires.

The Bible is replete with examples of compromise reflecting divine love. The story of Joseph, sold into slavery by his jealous brothers, demonstrates a profound act of forgiveness and compromise on Joseph's part. Despite the immense pain inflicted upon him, he chose compassion and reconciliation, ultimately saving his family from starvation. His actions, guided by divine grace, show how compromise, born from a heart filled with love, can transcend personal hurt and bring about miraculous reconciliation.

This resonates deeply with the message of **Matthew 5:44** , where Jesus commands us to *"love your enemies and pray for those who persecute you,"* a call for a radical form of compromise that counters human nature. Moreover, the concept of compromise finds its roots in the very nature of marriage, a union blessed by God and presented as a metaphor for the relationship between Christ and the church.

**Ephesians 5:22-33** describes a mutual submission between husband and wife, a reciprocal compromise where each partner willingly yields to the other's needs and desires. It's not about one partner dominating or subjugating the other, but a harmonious blending of wills, each contributing to the other's well-being and growth. This kind of compromise isn't about surrender; it's about selfless giving, a reflection of Christ's self-sacrificial love. It involves active listening, understanding each other's perspectives, and willingly choosing to prioritize the needs of the spouse above one's own preferences at times.

The application of this principle extends far beyond marital relations; it encompasses all familial connections. Parents frequently encounter situations requiring compromise. A child's insistent desire for a particular toy might conflict with the family budget; a teenager's desire for independence might challenge parental authority. However, through compassionate dialogue and willingness to find middle ground, parents can teach their children the value of compromise, modelling Christ-like love and laying the foundation for healthy relationships. A parent who rigidly adheres to their own preferences without considering their child's perspective risks creating resentment and damaging the parent-child bond. Conversely, a parent who compassionately considers their child's perspective, while ensuring boundaries are upheld, teaches valuable life lessons, fostering a strong and loving relationship. Furthermore, the siblings' relationship often demands compromise.

Competition for parental attention, possessions, or even simply differing personalities can lead to conflict. However, learning to compromise—sharing, taking turns, and considering each other's feelings—builds empathy and strengthens familial bonds. A sibling who consistently prioritizes their own desires over those of their brother or sister creates a climate of resentment and disharmony. Instead, through mutual compromise, a sense of unity and mutual respect can emerge, mimicking the unity within the body of Christ described in **1 Corinthians 12** . Compromise in these sibling relationships helps cultivate an environment where each member feels valued and loved, thereby promoting a harmonious family atmosphere.

The act of compromising, however, isn't merely about reaching a mutually agreeable solution. It is also about the process – the willingness to listen, empathize, and find common ground. It necessitates patience, understanding, and a commitment to respectful dialogue. It means putting aside one's own ego and focusing on building a stronger family unit. This involves recognizing the valid perspectives of other family members, even when those perspectives differ significantly from our own. It demands humility, a willingness to acknowledge that we may not always be right, and that others' needs and desires are equally valid.

Furthermore, compromise within the family should be approached with prayerful consideration. Seeking God's guidance helps us navigate complex situations, discern His will, and approach disagreements with a heart of love and compassion. Prayer fosters humility, allowing us to approach conversations with a spirit of openness and a willingness to compromise, guided by a higher power. It helps us remember the bigger picture—that our relationships are not just about us, but about reflecting God's love and grace in our actions and decisions. By praying for wisdom and guidance, we can ensure that our compromises align with God's will and contribute to the overall well-being of the family.

In conclusion, compromise in family life is not merely a practical tool for conflict resolution; it's an expression of love, an embodiment of selflessness, and a pathway to stronger, more meaningful relationships. By embracing compromise with a spirit of humility and love, we create a familial atmosphere that reflects the very essence of God's grace and compassion. It is through these acts of selfless giving that we truly build a family united in love,
mirroring the unity found within the body of Christ. The journey requires effort, patience, and understanding, but the rewards—a family bound by love, respect, and mutual support—are immeasurable, a testament to the transformative power of compromise rooted in faith and love.

It's a journey that strengthens not only our family bonds but also our relationship with God, reflecting His selfless love for humanity.

## Avoiding Power Struggles Through Compromise

The insidious nature of power struggles within families often stems from a lack of genuine compromise. It's a subtle erosion, a slow chipping away at the foundation of mutual respect and love, where each member seeks dominance rather than collaboration. This isn't about petty squabbles over remote control access; it's about deeply ingrained patterns of behavior that dictate who makes decisions, who holds the authority, and who ultimately feels valued and heard. The result? A family fractured by resentment, tension, and a pervasive sense of unfairness. But the good news is that this cycle can be broken. By embracing compromise as a fundamental principle, families can effectively dismantle these power dynamics and foster an environment of mutual respect and collaboration.

One of the most effective ways to preempt power struggles is through proactive communication. Open dialogue, where each family member feels safe to express their needs and desires without fear of judgment or ridicule, is crucial. Imagine a family deciding on a vacation destination. Instead of one parent dictating the choice, leading to resentment from the other, a collaborative  approach can be employed. Each member shares their preferences –perhaps one child dreams of a beach vacation, another yearns for a mountain adventure, while the parents envision a historical city exploration. Instead of a showdown, a compromise can be reached: a beach vacation with opportunities for hiking nearby, or a city exploration with time allocated for a day trip to the mountains. This demonstrates that the needs of each individual matter, promoting a sense of being valued and heard. The key is to listen actively, empathize with differing perspectives, and be willing to yield on certain points to achieve a mutually agreeable outcome.

This process requires a shift in mindset. We often fall into the trap of viewing compromise as a sign of weakness, a concession that diminishes our authority or importance. But viewed through a biblical lens, compromise is an act of love, mirroring the selfless sacrifice of Christ. Just as He laid down His life for us, willingly compromising His own comfort and desires, so too should we be willing to compromise within our families. It is an act of humbling ourselves, putting the needs of others ahead of our own. This doesn't mean relinquishing our values or compromising our integrity; rather, it is about finding creative solutions that honor the needs of everyone involved, respecting the individuality of each member.

Consider the parable of the talents in **Matthew 25**. Each servant received a different number of talents, reflecting individual abilities and strengths. Yet, the master praised those who diligently used their talents, regardless of the number received. This illustrates that compromise is not about equal contributions, but about equal effort and recognition of individual capacities. A parent might have more time to dedicate to household chores, while a child might excel at helping with yard work. Compromise acknowledges these differences and leverages them to achieve a shared goal: a well-functioning home environment. It is about working together, utilizing strengths and covering weaknesses, fostering mutual support and understanding.

Furthermore, compromise necessitates empathy and understanding. Before launching into a debate or conflict, take the time to truly understand the other person's perspective. Why is this issue so important to them? What are their underlying needs and concerns? By understanding their motivations, you can better appreciate their position, even if you don't agree with it. This empathetic approach fosters a sense of connection and mutual respect, paving the way for productive dialogue and compromise. It's a crucial aspect of building stronger family bonds, reflecting the love and understanding that should characterize our relationships with each other and with God.

Often, power struggles arise from unmet needs. A child constantly seeking attention might be demonstrating an unmet need for connection and validation. A parent consistently controlling decisions might be driven by a need for order and security. By identifying these underlying needs, families can address them directly, lessening the need for power struggles. Perhaps the attention-seeking child needs more one-on-one time with a parent. Or the controlling parent needshelp delegating tasks and trusting family members to contribute. Understanding these fundamental needs opens doors to solutions that go beyond superficial conflict resolution and address the root causes of the power struggle.

This requires honest self-reflection and a willingness to acknowledge our own vulnerabilities and needs.

The practical application of compromise requires setting clear expectations and boundaries. While compromise involves flexibility and willingness to adjust, it should not come at the cost of core values or personal boundaries. These boundaries, when established clearly and respectfully, provide a framework within which
compromises can be made without sacrificing personal well-being. For example, if a family is deciding on screen time limits, compromise can involve a negotiated schedule that balances the needs of each member while ensuring that healthy boundaries are maintained. The goal is not to eliminate all disagreements, but to navigate them constructively.

Furthermore, it's crucial to learn to forgive. Resentment festers, fueling future power struggles. When compromise falls short of expectations, or when one person feels unfairly treated, forgiveness becomes crucial in repairing the fractured relationship. Holding on to past grievances only perpetuates conflict. Forgiveness doesn't mean condoning hurtful behavior, but rather releasing the anger and bitterness that prevent healing and growth. This aligns perfectly with biblical teachings of forgiveness and reconciliation, essential for building strong, healthy relationships. The act of forgiving, rooted in a spirit of compassion and understanding, helps restore the trust necessary for future compromises.

Finally, prayer and seeking divine guidance are essential components of resolving family conflict through compromise. Seeking God's wisdom and perspective can illuminate blind spots, reveal underlying motivations, and guide us toward solutions that honor His principles. Prayer fosters humility, encouraging us to surrender our pride and seek solutions that place the well-being of others, and ultimately the glory of God, at the forefront. It aligns our desires with His, leading to outcomes that are not only mutually beneficial but also spiritually enriching. This is the cornerstone of true family harmony – a harmony built not on human strength, but on divine grace and guidance. By seeking God's wisdom and submitting to His will, families find the strength and guidance necessary to navigate conflict and embrace compromise, creating relationships that reflect His love and compassion.

The journey toward avoiding power struggles through compromise is not a quick fix, but a continuous process that requires dedication, patience, and a commitment to growth. It is a journey of self-reflection, learning to listen, and practicing empathy. But the rewards are immeasurable: a family united in love, respect, and mutual support, a family that mirrors the unity and love found within the body of Christ. It is in this unity that true fulfillment and lasting peace are found – a testament to the power of compromise rooted in faith, love, and a commitment to God's plan for our families.

The goal is not the absence of conflict but the ability to resolve conflict constructively and with love, reflecting the transformative power of a family united in Christ.

## *Chapter 5: Change: Adapting with Grace and Faith*

-*Embracing Change Navigating Life's Transitions*

-*Responding to Unexpected Circumstances*

-*Supporting Each Other Through Difficult Time*

-*Growth Through Adversity*

-*Adapting to Changing Family Dynamics*

## Embracing Change Navigating Lifes Transitions

Change is the only constant in life, a truth as undeniable as the rising and setting of the sun. This is especially true within the context of family life. From the joyous arrival of a new child to the bittersweet departure of a grown one, from unexpected illnesses to career shifts, and even the simple passage of time itself, families are perpetually in motion, navigating a sea of transitions. These transitions, though often challenging, offer opportunities for growth, strengthening the bonds of faith and love that hold a family together. The key lies in approaching change not with fear or resistance, but with grace and faith, understanding that God's hand guides us even amidst the upheaval.

The Bible is replete with examples of individuals and families who faced significant change. Consider the story of Abraham, called by God to leave his homeland and embark on a journey into the unknown. This was a profound change, a complete upheaval of his life, yet Abraham, through faith, obeyed. His obedience, his willingness to embrace the uncertainty, paved the way for a remarkable legacy, a testament to the power of faith in the face of profound change. His family, too, were transformed by this experience, learning to trust in God's provision and guidance in the face of the unknown.

Similarly, the Israelites' journey from slavery in Egypt to freedom in the Promised Land was a monumental transition. Forty years wandering in the wilderness, facing hunger, thirst, and the constant threat of enemies—this was not the easy path they had envisioned. Yet, through it all, God remained their constant companion, providing for their needs and guiding them toward their ultimate destination. Their experience is a powerful reminder that even the most arduous transitions can lead to blessings beyond our comprehension, provided we maintain faith in God's plan. In our own lives, we encounter change in countless ways.

A job loss can trigger feelings of anxiety and insecurity, threatening the family's financial stability. An unexpected illness can disrupt routines and cast a shadow of uncertainty over the future. The departure of a child to college can leave a void in the family dynamic, creating a sense of loss and adjustment for both parents and the child. These are all significant transitions that require us to adapt, to adjust our expectations, and to find new ways of being together.

But how do we navigate these changes with grace and faith? How do we maintain our family bonds amidst the storms of life? The answer, I believe, lies in several key principles. Firstly, we must acknowledge the reality of change, accepting that it is an inherent part of the human experience. Resistance only prolongs the pain and hinders our ability to move forward. By embracing change as an opportunity for growth, we open ourselves to new possibilities and blessings that might otherwise remain hidden. Secondly, we must maintain open and honest communication within the family.

Sharing our fears, anxieties, and hopes allows us to support each other and find strength in unity. When we create a space for vulnerability and empathy, we foster a sense of solidarity that enables us to face challenges together. This shared vulnerability, this act of mutual support, creates a powerful bond, reinforcing the family's resilience and ability to weather the storm.

Thirdly, prayer and faith are indispensable tools in navigating life's transitions. Turning to God in prayer, acknowledging His sovereignty and seeking His guidance, provides us with comfort, hope, and a sense of peace amidst uncertainty. Trusting in His plan, even when we don't understand it, frees us from the burden of carrying the weight of our anxieties alone. Remember, God doesn't promise an absence of storms, but He does promise to be with us through them.

Fourthly, we must remember that change often brings about opportunities for growth. Challenges force us to confront our weaknesses, to develop new skills, and to discover hidden strengths within ourselves and our family. They challenge us to grow spiritually, emotionally, and relationally. Embracing these opportunities, seeking to learn and adapt, is crucial in making change a source of strength, not just survival.

Consider a family facing a sudden job loss. The initial reaction might be panic and despair. However, by relying on their faith, they can turn to God for guidance and support. They might discover unexpected opportunities, perhaps leading to a more fulfilling career path or a stronger sense of community. The challenge, though initially devastating, could ultimately lead to unforeseen blessings and a renewed sense of purpose.

Or imagine a family adjusting to the departure of a child to college.While sadness is natural, focusing on the positive aspects – the child's growth and independence, the new opportunities for both the child and the remaining family members – can ease the transition. Maintaining regular communication, sharing in each other's lives, and celebrating milestones together can strengthen the family bond even amidst the change.

The process of adapting to change is not always easy. There will be moments of frustration, sadness, and even anger. It's important to acknowledge these emotions, allowing ourselves and our families to grieve the loss of what was, while simultaneously embracing the possibilities of what is to come. It's a journey, not a destination. We must be patient with ourselves and with each other, providing space for healing and growth. Remember, as followers of Christ, we are not alone in our struggles.

God is our constant companion, offering comfort, guidance, and strength throughout every transition. He walks with us through the valley of the shadow of death, and He leads us towards new beginnings. By embracing change with grace and faith, we can not only survive life's inevitable transitions, but thrive, growing stronger and closer as a family, our bonds deepened by the shared experiences we have overcome together. The trials we face, while difficult, serve to refine our faith and strengthen our reliance on God's unfailing love and grace. This is the journey of faith, the path towards deeper connection with God and with each other. It is a path that, though challenging, leads to an abundance of blessings, both seen and unseen.

## Responding to Unexpected Circumstances

Life, in its unpredictable nature, often throws curveballs. Just when we think we have a firm grasp on our routines, our plans, our carefully constructed sense of normalcy, something unexpected comes along to shake things up. A sudden job loss. A serious illness in the family. An unexpected relocation. These are not merely inconveniences; they are seismic shifts that can leave us reeling, questioning our faith, our stability, and our very sense of self. But even in the face of these unforeseen circumstances, our faith remains our anchor, our guiding light through the storm.

Consider the story of Job, a man whose life was shattered by a series of devastating misfortunes. His wealth was wiped out, his children perished, and his health deteriorated. Yet, through it all, Job maintained his faith in God, his unwavering belief in a higher power that ultimately provided comfort and meaning to his trials. His story serves as a powerful testament to the enduring strength of faith in the face of unimaginable adversity. Job's experience, though extreme, mirrors the smaller, yet equally challenging, unexpected circumstances that we face in our everyday lives. The loss of a job, for instance, can trigger a cascade of anxieties: financial insecurity, fear for the future, the potential strain on family relationships. These anxieties are entirely understandable, but they are not insurmountable.

Our response to these situations should not be one of panic or despair. Instead, we can choose to approach them with a spirit of faith, seeking guidance and strength from our Lord. Prayer becomes our lifeline, a direct connection to the divine source of comfort and wisdom. We pour out our anxieties, our fears, and our uncertainties before God, seeking His guidance on how to navigate the unexpected challenges that confront us.

Prayer is not merely a passive act; it's a powerful act of faith that engages God's intervention in our lives. It is an acknowledgement of our dependence on Him and a trust in His perfect plan, even if that plan remains hidden from our earthly perspectives. Beyond prayer, we must actively engage in practical steps to address the situation at hand. If it's a job loss, we seek support from friends, family, and even our church community. We actively search for new employment opportunities, leveraging our skills and networks to find a new path. This is not about resigning ourselves to fate; rather, it's about acting in faith, trusting that God will open doors and provide opportunities.

Remember the parable of the talents? God expects us to utilize the gifts and abilities He has given us to the best of our ability. Searching for a new job, honing existing skills, and developing new ones are ways we honor that trust and show our faith in His provision.Unexpected illnesses present another set of challenges. The emotional toll on both the patient and the family can be immense. Fear, uncertainty, and grief are natural reactions.

But in the midst of these difficult emotions, faith can serve as a balm, providing strength, hope, and perspective. We pray for healing, both physical and emotional. We rely on the support of our loved ones and seek medical advice, taking appropriate steps to care for the individual who is ill. We remember that even in sickness, God's love and grace extend to us. He walks with us, providing comfort and strength.

This does not always mean miraculous healing, but it does mean His unwavering presence and unfailing love, even amidst suffering.Relocation, whether planned or unplanned, can bring its own set of challenges. Leaving behind familiar surroundings, friends, and established routines can be unsettling. The adjustment period can be fraught with difficulties, requiring adaptation and resilience. Yet, even here, faith can provide guidance. We trust that God is leading us, even if we don't fully understand the reason for the change. We seek out new connections in our new community, making an effort to integrate ourselves and build a new support system.

This process of building new relationships demonstrates our faith in God's ability to provide for our needs and establish new meaningful connections.It's essential to remember that responding to unexpected circumstances is not solely a matter of practical strategies. It's also about cultivating a mindset of faith and resilience. This involves nurturing gratitude, focusing on the positive aspects of our lives, and actively choosing hope over despair. Even amidst the chaos and uncertainty, we can choose to find gratitude for the blessings we still have, and in doing so, strengthen our faith. Consider the experience of a family I counseled, the Millers. Their lives were thrown into turmoil when their small business, a family-run bakery, unexpectedly caught fire. They lost everything – their livelihood, their savings, and much of their equipment. The initial reaction was understandably devastating.

They felt despair and questioned their faith. But, through prayer and the support of their church community, they slowly began to rebuild. The church members rallied around them, providing financial assistance, temporary housing, and emotional support. The Millers, through their faith, found the strength to start again. They worked tirelessly, their faith serving as a motivator during long and difficult days. They eventually reopened their bakery, even bigger and better than before, a testament to their resilience and their unwavering faith in God's plan.

Another family I knew, the Joneses, faced a different

challenge. Their teenage daughter fell gravely ill, and the diagnosis was uncertain and frightening. The uncertainty gnawed at them, triggering intense anxiety and fear. But their faith anchored them. They prayed constantly for their daughter's healing, and they also sought the best medical care possible. They leaned on their faith, their friends, and their family for support. They found comfort in their shared faith and in the shared burden carried by the people who loved them.

While the outcome was not a complete recovery as they hoped for, their faith allowed them to adjust to a new reality, offering them a deeper, more meaningful appreciation for life and their family.

In these examples, the common thread is the unwavering faith of the families involved. Their faith didn't prevent the hardships, but it provided the strength, resilience, and perspective to navigate the difficult times. It's not about ignoring the pain or pretending everything is fine. It's about acknowledging the challenges, trusting in God's plan, even if that plan remains unclear, and actively seeking His guidance and strength. Through faith, prayer, and practical action, we can find a path forward, even amidst the most unexpected and challenging circumstances.

Remember, God is not absent in our trials; He is present, offering his comfort, guidance, and unwavering love. Our faith in Him is the key that unlocks His grace and helps us overcome even the most difficult of life's storms. It is a path of surrender and trust, a path that, though challenging, leads to a deeper relationship with God and a stronger, more resilient family unit. Furthermore, cultivating a strong support network is crucial.

Leaning on friends, family, and your church community provides emotional, practical, and spiritual sustenance during difficult times. Sharing your burdens with others reduces feelings of isolation and provides a sense of collective strength. Our faith communities are designed to support each other, sharing the burdens and offering encouragement and hope. It is in this shared experience of faith that our individual strength is amplified, providing a collaborative approach to navigating life's unexpected challenges.

In conclusion, responding to unexpected circumstances requires a multifaceted approach – a blend of faith, prayer, practical action, and the support of our community. It's about remembering that God's grace is sufficient and that even in the midst of uncertainty and hardship, we are not alone. He is our constant companion, our guiding light, and our source of unwavering strength. By embracing faith, we not only survive but thrive, emerging stronger and closer to God and to each other, our faith deepened and our family bonds strengthened by the trials we have overcome together. Our journey of faith, though full of twists and turns, leads to a richer and more profound relationship with our Creator, a relationship that becomes our anchor in life's unpredictable sea.

## Supporting Each Other Through Difficult Times

The unexpected storm clouds of life—job losses, illnesses, financial setbacks, relational rifts—often descend without warning. These aren't merely trials; they are tests of faith, resilience, and the very fabric of our family bonds. How we navigate these turbulent waters determines not only our individual survival but the strength and unity of our family unit. The scriptures are replete with examples of families facing hardship, and their responses offer valuable guidance. Consider the story of Job; his unwavering faith, even in the face of unimaginable loss, stands as a testament to the power of perseverance. Yet, it was also his family, his friends, though initially misguided in their approach, who offered him comfort and company through his ordeal.

Supporting one another during these difficult times isn't a passive endeavor; it requires active participation, thoughtful empathy, and a willingness to step outside of our comfort zones. It's not merely about offering platitudes; it's about embodying Christ's love in tangible ways. Practical support often makes the greatest difference. When a family member loses their job, a helping hand with childcare, meal preparation, or even financial assistance can be transformative. It acknowledges their burden and demonstrates tangible love, relieving some of the pressure and offering a lifeline in their moment of need.

The act itself transcends the monetary value; it speaks volumes about the commitment and support of the family unit.

Beyond the practical, emotional support is crucial. Active listening, a willingness to simply be present without judgment, and the offering of a comforting presence can be invaluable. Sometimes, simply holding space for someone to express their pain, fear, or anger without interruption is the most significant act of support we can offer. Remembering that emotional pain is as valid as physical pain helps us to empathize more deeply. The Bible teaches us the importance of bearing one another's burdens **(Galatians 6:2)**.

This isn't about taking away someone's struggles, but about sharing the weight, lessening the load, and offering a comforting presence in the midst of turmoil. Spiritual support, intertwined with emotional and practical support, forms the bedrock of a family's resilience. Prayer, both individual and shared, can be a powerful source of strength and comfort. Gathering together for prayer, sharing scriptures that offer solace and hope, and reminding each other of God's unwavering love and promises can be deeply restorative.

These acts of spiritual support aren't simply about religious ritual; they are about actively seeking God's guidance and strength as a family, uniting in faith to navigate the challenges together. Remember the Psalms, filled with expressions of lament, sorrow, and ultimate trust in God's faithfulness. Sharing these with each other, acknowledging shared struggles and seeking solace in God's promises, builds a stronger spiritual foundation for the family. Let me share a story from my counseling experience.

A family I worked with experienced a devastating house fire, losing all their possessions. The initial reaction was understandably one of despair and disorientation. Yet, the remarkable thing was how the family rallied around each other.

The adult children immediately moved back home, temporarily sacrificing their own lives and comforts to support their parents. Neighbors and church members offered practical help, providing clothing, food, and temporary housing. But more importantly, they provided emotional support, offering a listening ear, a shoulder to cry on, and a constant presence of love and compassion. They held prayer meetings, offering spiritual comfort and reaffirming their shared faith in God's provision. This wasn't a quick fix; it was a long, arduous process. Yet, by supporting each other through thick and thin, they not only rebuilt their home, but they rebuilt their faith and strengthened their family bonds in ways they could never have imagined.

Another example demonstrates the power of forgiveness in strengthening family ties during difficult times. A family I know experienced a significant rift when a family member made a grave mistake that deeply hurt others. Instead of engaging in blame and recrimination, the family chose a path of forgiveness and reconciliation. This was a process that took time, requiring humility, empathy, and a willingness to understand the other's perspective. The path to forgiveness wasn't easy, demanding honesty, open communication, and a recognition of shared humanity. But the willingness to forgive, to extend grace, and to work through the pain together strengthened the family's foundation and ultimately led to a more profound sense of unity and understanding. The process involved prayer, seeking spiritual guidance to understand the importance of forgiveness as Christ taught and practiced.

The importance of communication cannot be overstated. Open, honest, and respectful communication forms the cornerstone of a supportive family unit. During challenging times, it is crucial to create a safe space where family members can openly express their feelings, fears, and concerns without judgment or criticism. Active listening, empathy, and a willingness to validate each other's emotions are essential components of healthy communication.Remember, communication isn't just about talking; it's about understanding. It's about creating a space where each member feels heard, valued, and supported. During times of crisis, this open communication often helps identify resources, needs, and ways each member can contribute to the family's overall well-being. The family becomes a united team working towards a shared goal.

Furthermore, the practice of forgiveness is essential to navigating difficult times. Holding onto resentment, anger, or bitterness only exacerbates the pain and weakens the family bonds. Forgiveness, while challenging, is a transformative act that releases both the giver and the receiver from the burden of past hurts. It doesn't mean condoning the wrong, but rather choosing to release the anger and resentment that prevents healing. This is where faith plays a crucial role. God's grace teaches us the power of forgiveness, and embracing this grace allows us to extend forgiveness to others and ourselves. Seeking forgiveness, offering it, and actively engaging in this process through prayer and reflection nurtures resilience and healing within the family unit.

Finally, remembering to prioritize self-care amidst the chaos is crucial. It's easy to become overwhelmed and depleted when supporting loved ones through difficult times. But neglecting our own well-being only diminishes our capacity to support others. Setting aside time for prayer, meditation, exercise, or simply quiet reflection can help replenish our emotional reserves. It's not selfish to prioritize self-care; it's an essential act of self-preservation that allows us to continue offering support without burning out. As the saying goes, "you can't pour from an empty cup."

Taking care of our physical and spiritual well-being enables us to be more present, compassionate, and effective in our support of our family members. In essence, our well-being becomes integral to our capacity to provide effective and compassionate support. This holistic approach—emotional, practical, spiritual, and personal self-care—underpins the family's capacity to weather any storm.

The love, support, and faith we share are not merely abstract concepts; they are the tangible lifeline that strengthens us, unites us, and carries us through life's most difficult times. The bonds formed through these trials are unbreakable, deeply rooted in faith and strengthened by shared experiences. This is the true essence of family – a sanctuary of love, support, and unwavering faith in the face of life's inevitable storms.

## Growth Through Adversity

The unexpected trials life throws our way—the sudden job loss, the crippling illness, the agonizing relational fracture—often feel less like tests and more like violent storms ripping through the very foundations of our existence. These aren't simply obstacles; they are crucibles, forging our faith, refining our resilience, and profoundly reshaping the dynamics of our families. The manner in which we navigate these turbulent seas determines not only our individual survival but, more significantly, the strength and the very essence of our family's unity.

The scriptures offer a wealth of examples of families grappling with profound hardship. Their responses, their resilience, and their ultimate triumphs provide a roadmap for us to follow. Consider the family of Joseph, a story etched in the **book of Genesis** . Joseph's brothers, driven by jealousy and resentment, sold him into slavery. The ensuing years saw Joseph unjustly imprisoned, yet through it all, his unwavering faith in God's plan remained steadfast.

His subsequent rise to power in Egypt, a position that ultimately saved his family from starvation, stands as a testament to the transformative power of adversity. The suffering he endured, the betrayal he faced, forged in him a strength and wisdom that benefited his entire family.

Their initial actions sowed seeds of discord, but the eventual reunion was a testament to God's restorative grace and the enduring power of family. This story underscores that the seemingly insurmountable obstacles life presents aren't necessarily roadblocks, but rather detours designed to lead us to a deeper understanding of ourselves, our relationships, and ultimately, our faith.

The story of Job, often cited as a quintessential example of unwavering faith in the face of immense suffering, resonates deeply with this concept. Job's loss—his possessions, his health, his children—was catastrophic. Yet, his unwavering faith, his refusal to curse God, is a powerful demonstration of spiritual resilience. While his friends' initial responses were misguided, offering platitudes rather than genuine comfort, Job's steadfastness ultimately serves as a beacon of hope.

The rebuilding of his life, the restoration of his family, and his increased wisdom after this trial showcase God's restorative power and the possibility of profound growth amidst suffering. Job's story isn't just about enduring hardship; it's about emerging from it stronger, wiser, and more deeply connected to God and his loved ones.

However, the path to growth through adversity isn't always a linear one. It's rarely a simple narrative of unwavering faith leading to immediate, miraculous resolution. The journey is often fraught with doubt, fear, anger, and even despair. It's perfectly acceptable, even necessary, to acknowledge and process these emotions. Suppressing them only hinders our healing process and prevents genuine growth. Open, honest communication within the family becomes paramount during these challenging times. Creating a safe space where each family member can express their feelings without judgment is essential. This requires empathy, active listening, and a willingness to put aside our own immediate needs to understand and validate the emotions of others.

This is where the importance of prayer and faith truly shines. Prayer isn't merely a passive act of asking God for help; it's a dynamic conversation, a lifeline to connect with divine strength and guidance. During times of adversity, prayer offers solace, perspective, and a renewed sense of hope. It allows us to surrender our anxieties to God, trusting in His plan, even when we cannot comprehend it. Moreover, faith is not a shield against suffering but a compass guiding us through it. It's the unwavering belief that even in the darkest of times, God is with us, working all things for our good **(Romans 8:28)**.

This belief isn't about avoiding suffering, but about finding meaning and purpose within it. Consider the example of the Israelites during their exodus from Egypt. Their journey through the wilderness was marked by
hardship, hunger, thirst, and constant challenges. Yet, amidst these trials, their faith in God was tested and strengthened. They witnessed God's miraculous provision, His unwavering faithfulness, and His enduring love. Their experiences in the desert ultimately forged a stronger sense of community and a deeper dependence on God. Their shared struggles, their collective reliance on God's grace, bound them together in ways that mere prosperity never could. Furthermore, adversity often reveals hidden strengths and capabilities within individuals and families. It forces us to rely on each other, to collaborate, and to discover unexpected reservoirs of resilience. Facing challenges together cultivates empathy, compassion, and a deeper appreciation for one another's strengths.

A family facing a shared hardship, such as a serious illness, often finds new levels of intimacy and support that might not have developed otherwise. The shared experience creates an unbreakable bond, a testament to their resilience and the strength of their family unit. In essence, the crucible of hardship refines and strengthens the bonds that hold a family together.

However, the growth that emerges from adversity isn't always immediately apparent. The process of healing and growth takes time; it's a gradual unfolding, a slow but steady transformation.There will be setbacks, moments of doubt, and times when we question our faith. But it's during these moments that we must remember the importance of patience and perseverance. We must trust that God is working in our lives, even when we cannot see the immediate results. Growth through suffering is a process, not a destination, a journey of faith that ultimately deepens our understanding of ourselves and our relationship with God and one another.

The process of navigating these challenges also offers opportunities for self-reflection and spiritual growth. When faced with adversity, we are often forced to confront our own weaknesses, our limitations, and our reliance on external validation. This self-awareness, often painful, is essential for genuine growth. It allows us to identify areas where we need to change, where we need to grow in faith, and where we need to rely more fully on God's grace. The introspection born from hardship can lead to a more profound and authentic relationship with God.

Furthermore, fostering forgiveness within the family is crucial. During times of adversity, resentments and hurts can easily fester, poisoning relationships and hindering healing. Forgiveness, however, isn't merely an act of letting go; it's a powerful act of releasing bitterness and creating space for love and reconciliation.

Forgiveness allows us to break free from the chains of anger and resentment, enabling us to move forward with renewed hope and purpose. It allows us to reconcile not only with each other but also with ourselves. The act of forgiving, both ourselves and others, is essential for healing and growth within the family. It is a fundamental act of spiritual maturity.

The concept of compromise, often seen as a sign of weakness, becomes essential in weathering adversity. It's a recognition that we're not always right, that we need to adapt and find common ground in the face of challenges.

Compromise requires flexibility, a willingness to bend, and a spirit of cooperation. In a family facing adversity, compromise isn't about surrendering our values, but about finding creative solutions that accommodate everyone's needs and concerns.

It fosters unity and cooperation, and prevents resentment from taking root. In conclusion, the journey through adversity is not one to be feared but embraced. It's an opportunity for spiritual and relational growth, a chance to strengthen family bonds and deepen our faith in God's unwavering love and grace. The trials we face, though painful, ultimately serve to refine us, making us stronger, wiser, and more resilient.

By embracing these challenges with faith, perseverance, and a spirit of unity, we not only survive but emerge transformed, our families bound together in a way that surpasses any hardship life might throw our way. The storms may rage, but the love that binds a family, rooted in faith, will see them through. The tapestry of family life, richly interwoven with shared trials and triumphs, becomes a masterpiece of resilience, faith, and enduring love.

## Adapting to Changing Family Dynamics

The transition from one season of life to another within a family is rarely seamless. It's more akin to navigating a winding river, sometimes gliding smoothly, other times battling rapids and unexpected currents. These transitions, often marked by significant life events, can profoundly alter the dynamics of family life. Children leaving for college or embarking on independent lives, aging parents requiring increasing care, the complexities of blended families – these are just a few of the currents that can test the resilience and unity of even the strongest family unit. Yet, within these challenges lies the potential for profound growth, deeper understanding, and a strengthening of the bonds that unite us.

Consider the poignant moment when a child, once nestled securely within the family cocoon, spreads their wings and flies. This is a joyous occasion, a testament to years of nurturing and guidance. However, it also marks a significant shift in family dynamics. The quiet hum of daily routines is disrupted; familiar roles and responsibilities are redefined. The silence that once felt empty may now feel deafening, a stark reminder of the void left behind. For parents, this transition can evoke a complex mix of emotions: pride, sorrow, anxiety, and even a sense of loss. The feeling is not unlike releasing a precious bird from its cage, a bittersweet ache in the heart knowing the journey ahead might lead them far away.

Adapting to this new reality requires a conscious effort to redefine the family's identity. It's not about replacing the child's presence but about carving out a new space for both the child and the parent to thrive. Open communication is paramount. Parents should proactively engage their children in conversations about their expectations and concerns. Encourage regular contact, whether through phone calls, video chats, or visits. Remember, the emotional connection doesn't diminish simply because physical proximity changes.

Furthermore, this is a valuable opportunity for parents to re-evaluate their own relationship. With children grown, many couples find themselves with more time for each other, a time to reconnect and reignite the spark that may have dimmed amidst the demands of raising a family. This is a period to rediscover shared interests, to embark on new adventures together, and to strengthen the emotional intimacy that forms the bedrock of a lasting partnership. This time, dedicated to cultivating a deeper connection, will help navigate any loneliness or adjustment issues. Remember to maintain individual hobbies and passions. It's not about merging into one entity, but rather about becoming two stronger individuals
complementing and supporting each other in this new stage.

The challenges presented by aging parents are equally complex. The roles often reverse, with children now providing care and support to their aging parents. This transition necessitates patience, compassion, and a willingness to adapt to the changing needs of both parties.
Open and honest conversations about medical and financial matters are crucial to ensure a smooth transition. While respecting their autonomy, a supportive plan should be in place to address practical issues.

The dynamic shifts significantly when managing medical or financial needs of aging parents. This is often not just a challenge for the adult children but may put a strain on the sibling relationships too. It's important to approach these challenges with empathy and understanding, recognizing the emotional toll it may take on everyone involved. Open communication among siblings is key to ensuring fair and equitable distribution of responsibilities and resources. Consider family meetings where everyone can express their feelings, concerns, and contributions. Mediation from an objective third party might be beneficial if tensions arise.

Remember, this isn't just about practical solutions; it's about honoring the legacy of your parents and maintaining a strong familial bond during a vulnerable time. Blended families present a unique set of complexities. Integrating two separate family units requires a delicate balance of respect, compromise, and a willingness to build new traditions and relationships. Establishing clear communication channels is critical. Family meetings, where everyone's voice is heard and valued, can foster a sense of belonging and shared purpose. Patience and understanding are crucial, as it takes time to build trust and navigate the emotional complexities of a new family structure. The focus should be on creating a supportive environment where each family member feels loved and respected.

Creating new family traditions can be a powerful way to foster unity and togetherness. Perhaps it's a weekly family dinner, a yearly holiday celebration, or a shared hobby or outing. These traditions create shared memories and a sense of belonging that transcend the individual family units. It is important to integrate the traditions from both families rather than eliminating the ones from the "other" family. The children need to feel their family customs are being respected. This fosters a sense of belonging and helps them to adapt and accept the new dynamics.

In addition to adapting to changing roles and responsibilities, it's crucial to address potential conflicts that may arise. Disagreements are inevitable, but learning to manage conflict constructively is crucial for maintaining strong family relationships. Encourage open communication, active listening, and a willingness to find mutually acceptable solutions. Mediation, either from a trusted family member or a professional counselor, may be beneficial in resolving particularly challenging conflicts. Remember, the goal is not to eliminate conflict but to navigate it in a way that strengthens the bonds of family.

Remember the importance of faith during these transitions. Leaning on your faith and the support of your faith community can offer comfort, guidance, and strength during challenging times. Prayer, scripture study, and participation in faith-based activities can provide a source of solace and inspiration. Remembering that God is our constant companion in times of challenge allows us to navigate the difficulties with more grace. Turning to your faith community for support and encouragement can build resilience and allow for the support needed to strengthen the family unit.

The scriptures offer abundant guidance on navigating family dynamics. **Proverbs 17:6** reminds us that *"Children's children are the crown of old men; and the glory of children are their fathers."*

This verse highlights the importance of intergenerational connections and the blessings that come from nurturing strong family relationships across different generations. Similarly, **Ephesians 5:22-33** emphasizes the importance of mutual respect and submission within the family unit. These principles provide a solid framework for navigating the complexities of family life, particularly during times of significant transition.

The journey of adapting to changing family dynamics is not a sprint; it is a marathon. It requires patience, understanding, and a willingness to embrace the evolving nature of family relationships. By prioritizing communication, fostering understanding, and leaning on our faith, we can navigate these transitions with grace and emerge with stronger, more resilient family bonds. The strength of a family lies not in its ability to avoid change but in its ability to adapt to change gracefully, maintaining the loving foundation that binds its members. The changes we face, while challenging, can forge a deeper connection, creating an even stronger, more resilient family structure. Embrace the journey and remember, your faith community is a great source of support and strength throughout the process. God's grace is sufficient for every challenge and every transition, transforming them into opportunities for growth and deeper connection.

## Chapter 6: A Wholehearted Approach to Faith, Family, and Relationships

-*Surrender and Trust Embracing Gods Will*

-*Living a Life of Purpose and Meaning*

-*The Blessings of Obedience and Faithfulness*

-*The Importance of Submissive Acts*

-*A Call to Wholehearted Living*

## Surrender and Trust Embracing Gods Will

The wind whispers secrets through the leaves, a gentle reminder of the unseen hand guiding our lives. Surrender. The word itself can feel daunting, even frightening. To surrender is to relinquish control, to step away from the reins and trust the journey to a power far greater than ourselves. But in the context of faith, family, and relationships, surrender is not weakness; it's the ultimate act of strength, a profound declaration of trust in a loving God.

Think of a small child, learning to ride a bicycle. Initially, they grip the handlebars with white knuckles, eyes fixed rigidly on the path ahead, terrified of falling. Their focus is entirely on maintaining balance, on controlling every movement. But the true joy of cycling, the freedom and exhilaration, comes only when they begin to relax, to trust their own instincts, and to let the bicycle guide them. Surrendering to the bike's momentum, they find a new level of grace and ease. Similarly, surrendering to God's will doesn't mean passive resignation; it's an active choice to trust His guidance, even when the path ahead is unclear.

The Bible is replete with examples of surrender leading to unexpected blessings. Consider Abraham, called to leave his homeland and journey to an unknown land, promised only a future he couldn't comprehend.

His act of faith, his surrender to God's command, became the foundation for a nation. He didn't know the "why" behind God's plan; he simply obeyed. His obedience, his surrender, became a testament to the transformative power of trust.

Or consider Joseph, sold into slavery by his brothers, falsely accused and imprisoned, yet through it all, maintaining his faith and integrity. His story is not one of passive acceptance but of active surrender – surrendering his understanding to God's plan, even when it felt utterly unjust. His unwavering faith, his refusal to allow bitterness or resentment to consume him, ultimately led him to a position of power, enabling him to save his family from famine.His journey underscores the idea that surrender isn't about avoiding hardship; it's about navigating hardship with faith and finding purpose even amidst suffering.

The beauty of surrender lies in the release it offers. It frees us from the burden of trying to control every aspect of our lives, from the relentless pressure of striving for perfection. It's an acknowledgement that we are not in control, that there is a higher power orchestrating our lives, guiding us towards a future we can only glimpse. And in that surrender, we discover a peace that surpasses all understanding.

In the context of family life, surrender means releasing the need to control our children, our spouses, even our own emotions. It's about trusting God to work in their lives, to guide them on their own paths, even when those paths diverge from our own expectations.

It's about leting go of our need for immediate results, our desire to micromanage every interaction, and trusting that God is actively involved in shaping and guiding our family dynamics. This doesn't imply neglecting our responsibilities; rather, it means fulfilling those responsibilities with a spirit of trust and a heart open to God's guidance.

Surrender also involves surrendering our anxieties and fears to God. When faced with challenges, when confronted with uncertainty, it's easy to succumb to panic and doubt. But surrendering our anxieties to God allows us to find strength and resilience in Him. **Psalm 55:22** assures us, "Cast all your anxiety on him because he cares for you." This isn't a passive act; it's an active casting, a conscious decision to relinquish our fears to a

God who is able and willing to bear our burdens.

In relationships, surrender is about releasing the need for control, for constant reassurance, for perfect compatibility. It's about accepting our partners for who they are, flaws and all, recognizing that true love involves a willingness to accept imperfections and to navigate differences with grace and understanding. It's about choosing to love unconditionally, even when it's difficult, knowing that true love is a reflection of God's own unconditional love. This isn't to say that surrender is easy. It's a daily practice, a continuous process of letting go and trusting.

There will be moments of doubt, moments of fear, moments when the path ahead feels shrouded in darkness. But it is in those moments that our faith is tested, our trust strengthened. And it is in those moments that we discover the profound peace and fulfillment that come from surrendering our will to God's.

The process of surrender requires a conscious decision, a willingness to step outside our comfort zones and embrace the unknown. It often involves actively seeking God's guidance through prayer, scripture, and fellowship with other believers. It requires humility, recognizing our own limitations and acknowledging God's infinite wisdom and power. It's a constant dialogue with God, a continuous process of seeking His guidance and surrendering to His plan. This involves listening to the quiet promptings of the Spirit, allowing God to gently guide our decisions and shape our actions.

One powerful way to cultivate surrender is through consistent prayer. Prayer isn't just a request list; it's a conversation, a communion with God. It's an opportunity to pour out our hearts, to share our anxieties and fears, and to actively seek God's wisdom and guidance. Through prayer, we develop a deeper relationship with God, strengthening our trust in His plan for our lives and our families. Regular Bible study further reinforces this trust, revealing God's character, His promises, and His unwavering love for us. Surrender is not a one-time event, but a continuous process, a lifelong journey of faith and trust.

The path of surrender is not always straightforward. There will be times when doubt creeps in, when fear threatens to overwhelm us. These are opportunities to practice our surrender, to cling to the promises of God, and to remember His faithfulness throughout our lives. We may not always understand God's plan, but we can trust in His goodness, His love, and His ultimate purpose for our lives. And in that trust, we find a deep and abiding peace, a peace that anchors us amidst life's storms. As we navigate the complexities of faith, family, and relationships, let us embrace the transformative power of surrender.

Let us choose to trust in God's plan, even when it's difficult to see the path ahead. Let us release our anxieties, our fears, our need for control, and find freedom in the embrace of God's sovereignty. In that surrender, we discover a joy, a peace, and a fulfillment that surpasses all understanding. The journey of faith is not a solo expedition; it's a shared journey, guided by a loving God who walks beside us every step of the way. Embrace the journey, and discover the profound blessing of surrender.

## Living a Life of Purpose and Meaning

The gentle rustling of leaves, a constant companion throughout our journey of faith, now seems to whisper a different message: a call to purpose. Surrender, as we've explored, is not passive resignation, but an active choice to align our lives with God's will. This alignment, this conscious decision to walk hand-in-hand with Him, is the cornerstone of living a life filled with purpose and meaning, impacting not only our individual journeys but also the tapestry of our family relationships.

Imagine a farmer tending his field. He doesn't haphazardly scatter seeds; he plants them with intention, knowing the potential for harvest. Similarly, our lives are not random occurrences; we are called to cultivate our lives with intentionality, guided by the divine gardener. This intentional living, rooted in faith, blossoms into a life rich with purpose. It's not about a relentless pursuit of achievement, but a gentle, persistent tending of the soul, nurtured by prayer, strengthened by scripture, and guided by the Holy Spirit.

The Bible is replete with examples of individuals who found their purpose through unwavering faith. Consider Joseph, sold into slavery by his brothers, yet he rose to become a powerful figure in Egypt, preserving his family during a devastating famine. His unwavering faith, even in the darkest of times, propelled him toward a purpose that transcended his personal suffering and ultimately saved his family. His story is a powerful testament to the fact that God often uses our trials to shape our purpose and refine our character. It's in the crucible of hardship that we often discover our truest strength and our deepest connection to God.

Similarly, consider the unwavering faith of Ruth. Her loyalty to her mother-in-law Naomi, even in the face of hardship and uncertainty, led her to a new life and a remarkable lineage. Her story teaches us that choosing to remain faithful, even when the path seems unclear, can lead to unexpected blessings and a profound sense of purpose.

Ruth's story isn't just about finding a husband; it's about unwavering loyalty, dedication, and trust in God's providence – a powerful model of how faith directs our purpose. Her life illustrates that our purpose isn't always grand or widely recognized; it often resides in the small, everyday acts of love and faithfulness.

But how does this faith-filled purpose translate into a meaningful family life? The answer lies in the practical application of biblical principles within the home. A family grounded in faith isn't a perfect, idealized portrait; it's a community of imperfect people striving towards a common goal – glorifying God and loving one another. This pursuit requires intentional effort, conscious decisions to prioritize faith, and consistent communication. Family meals, for instance, become more than just sustenance; they become opportunities for prayer, sharing, and connection.

Regular family devotions, even short ones, can create a sacred space where faith is openly discussed and celebrated. These seemingly simple acts cultivate a spiritual atmosphere that fosters a sense of belonging, security, and shared purpose. Children learn the importance of faith not through lectures, but through observation and experience – witnessing their parents' commitment to prayer, scripture, and service.

Furthermore, living a life of purpose naturally spills over into our relationships beyond the family unit. Our faith informs our interactions with friends, colleagues, and even strangers. It compels us to act with kindness, compassion, and forgiveness, reflecting the love of Christ in our daily lives. Our purpose is not confined to the walls of our homes; it extends outward, influencing the world around us.

This outward expression of faith might involve volunteering at a local soup kitchen, mentoring a young person, or simply offering a listening ear to someone in need. The acts themselves are not as important as the motivation behind them – a genuine desire to serve others out of a heart filled with God's love. This outward focus, rooted in our inner purpose, brings a profound sense of fulfillment and joy that transcends personal gain.

However, the journey towards living a purposeful life is not without its challenges. Doubt, fear, and discouragement are inevitable. These are not signs of failure, but opportunities for growth. The key is to lean on God during these difficult times, trusting in His unwavering love and guidance. Just as a vine clings to a trellis for support, we must cling to God during times of uncertainty, allowing His strength to sustain us.

Consider David, the shepherd boy who became king. His life was filled with trials and tribulations, yet his unwavering faith in God enabled him to overcome adversity and ultimately fulfill his God-given purpose. He faced giants, betrayal, and persecution, yet his relationship with God remained his anchor, his source of strength and guidance. David's Psalms are a testament to his struggles and his triumphs, a poignant reminder that even in the darkest of times, God's love and faithfulness remain constant.

Our lives, like David's, will inevitably contain moments of darkness and despair. But it is through these trials that our faith is tested and refined, our character strengthened, and our purpose clarified. Embrace the challenges, knowing that God is using them to shape you, to prepare you for the greater purpose

He has in store for you.

Remember, the pursuit of purpose is a lifelong journey, not a destination. It's a dynamic process of growth, learning, and adaptation. There will be moments of clarity and moments of confusion, times of triumph and times of setback. But through it all, maintaining a Christ-centered perspective will illuminate the path forward, guiding our steps and giving meaning to our experiences.

Living a life of purpose and meaning is not about achieving some abstract ideal of perfection. It's about striving to live a life that reflects God's love, grace, and mercy. It's about aligning our actions with our beliefs, allowing our faith to shape our choices and motivate our actions. It's about finding joy in the journey, celebrating the small victories, and learning from the setbacks.

It's about embracing our imperfections and trusting in God's grace to transform us into the people He created us to be. And in that transformation, we discover not just our individual purpose, but also the transformative power of a family united in faith, love, and shared purpose – a family reflecting God's glory in the world. The journey, though challenging at times, is ultimately one of immense reward, leading to a life overflowing with purpose, meaning, and the profound joy that comes from walking hand-in-hand with our Creator.

## The Blessings of Obedience and Faithfulness

The whispering leaves, once a symbol of the quiet surrender required for a purposeful life, now seem to sing a triumphant song—a hymn to the abundant blessings that flow from obedience and faithfulness. Surrender, we've learned, isn't passive; it's an active participation in God's grand design, a dance of trust where our will aligns with His. This alignment, this unwavering commitment to His path, isn't merely a personal endeavor; it profoundly impacts the fabric of our families, weaving together threads of love, resilience, and a shared journey toward spiritual growth.

Consider the family of Abraham, a patriarch whose life stands as a testament to the transformative power of obedience. His willingness to leave his homeland, to journey into an unknown future guided solely by God's promise, set in motion a lineage that would shape the history of nations. While his journey was fraught with challenges—periods of doubt, moments of testing, and the agonizing uncertainties of faith —his unwavering obedience laid the foundation for a family marked by profound blessings.

The covenant God made with Abraham, sealed through obedience, reverberates through generations, a promise of protection, prosperity, and a future rooted in God's faithfulness. His descendants, though they stumbled and fell, inherited the rich legacy of a heritage built on faith and the unwavering commitment to God's will. The very existence of the nation of Israel is a testament to the ripple effect of Abraham's obedience, demonstrating how one family's faithfulness can have global implications.

Abraham's story is a mirror reflecting the principle that obedience isn't a mere obligation; it's a pathway to unprecedented blessings. It's not about earning God's favor; rather, it's about aligning ourselves with His perfect plan, allowing His wisdom and grace to guide our steps. The blessings aren't always immediate, nor are they always easily recognizable. Sometimes, the blessings are the lessons learned in the midst of trials, the growth experienced in the crucible of adversity, the deepened faith forged in the fires of testing.

Abraham's journey teaches us that true blessings encompass farmore than material possessions or earthly success; they encompass a relationship with God that transcends time, a legacy that echoes across generations, and a spiritual richness that endures forever.

Consider, too, the family of Joseph. His story, woven with threads of betrayal, imprisonment, and unexpected elevation, showcases the profound impact of faithfulness even in the face of unimaginable hardship. Joseph's unwavering commitment to his values, his steadfast refusal to compromise his integrity, even when faced with the ultimate temptation, paved the way for his extraordinary destiny. His faithfulness didn't shield him from suffering; it transformed his suffering into a means of saving his family and his people from famine. His story underscores a powerful truth: faithfulness, often tested in the crucible of adversity, brings forth unforeseen blessings, demonstrating God's sovereign hand in shaping even the darkest of circumstances. His remarkable journey from a despised son to the savior of his family highlights the transformative power of faith and its ability to weave beauty from ashes.

The unwavering faith and obedience of Joseph's father, Jacob, though initially flawed, ultimately transformed into a life marked by both repentance and a deepened reliance on God's grace. Jacob's wrestling match with God at Peniel signifies a pivotal moment of surrender, a turning point from cunning manipulation to a heartfelt reliance on divine guidance. This pivotal spiritual encounter shaped not only his life but also the lives of his descendants.

The blessings that flowed from Jacob's eventual submission to God's will are evident in the growth and prosperity of his family, and the eventual establishment of the twelve tribes of Israel—a testament to the long-term consequences of faith, repentance, and commitment to God's plan. His life demonstrates that even a life marked by initial struggles and flawed choices can find redemption and experience the rich blessings that arise from repentance, obedience, and faithfulness to God's will.

The **Book of Proverbs** is replete with wisdom regarding the blessings that flow from obedience and the devastating consequences of disobedience.

Verse after verse emphasizes the importance of honoring parents, submitting to authority, and walking in integrity. These principles, though seemingly simple, form the bedrock of strong families and thriving communities.

Families built on obedience experience a deeper sense of unity, mutual respect, and a shared commitment to common values. The blessing of a cohesive family is immeasurable, offering love, support, and stability in the face of life's inevitable challenges. It creates a safe haven where individual members feel cherished, protected, and empowered to pursue their own unique paths under the loving guidance of a united family.

But obedience is not simply a matter of blind conformity; it's a conscious choice to align our lives with God's will as revealed in His Word and through the promptings of the Holy Spirit. It involves actively seeking His guidance, discerning His purpose for our lives and our families, and having the courage to follow His path even when it's difficult or unclear. It requires humility, recognizing our limitations and acknowledging God's sovereignty over all aspects of our lives. True obedience isn't robotic compliance; it's a heartfelt response of love and trust.

Obedience, however, does not preclude challenges. The lives of faithful individuals in scripture often reveal a pattern of trials, tests, and even suffering. The families of Job, David, and even Jesus himself faced immense hardship. But these trials, far from contradicting the blessings of obedience, often served to refine their faith, deepen their dependence on God, and ultimately, reveal the depth and extent of God's love and grace. These trials are not punishments for disobedience, but often opportunities for spiritual growth, refining the character and strengthening the faith of those who remain steadfast in their commitment to God.

The story of Job, though painful, demonstrates the unwavering faithfulness of a man who, despite the loss of everything, maintained his integrity and refused to curse God. His unwavering faith, amidst unimaginable suffering, ultimately resulted in a restoration far beyond anything he could have imagined. His perseverance, his relentless faith, serves as a powerful testament to the blessings that come to those who endure with steadfast hearts, even when the path seems impossibly difficult. This is a profound lesson of hope, showing how faithfulness endures even the fiercest storms, resulting in an even deeper relationship with God and a rich reward in the end.

Furthermore, the example of David, though a man of great faith, was not without his flaws. His life demonstrates that even those who strive to live in obedience will make mistakes. However, David's repentance, his heartfelt confession, and his sincere turning back to God serve as a powerful reminder that God's grace is always available to those who humbly acknowledge their failings and seek His forgiveness. His life teaches us that the path of obedience is not one of flawless perfection, but rather a continual journey of striving, failing, repenting, and seeking God's strength to overcome the inevitable challenges and shortcomings we face. His willingness to be corrected, and his commitment to returning to God's favor, highlight the importance of humility and ongoing repentance within the process of growing in faith and obedience.

The blessings of obedience and faithfulness are not limited to the individual; they extend to the family and beyond. Families who prioritize spiritual growth, who commit to prayer, Bible study, and mutual support, experience a greater sense of unity, peace, and resilience. These families are better equipped to navigate the inevitable storms of life, knowing that their foundation is built on a solid rock—the unyielding love and grace of God. The children raised in such families inherit a precious legacy of faith, values, and a sense of belonging that shapes their lives in profound ways. It's not just about outward displays of religious practice; it's about cultivating a heart posture of love, submission, and a willingness to yield to the guidance of the Holy Spirit in every aspect of family life.

In conclusion, the path of obedience and faithfulness is a path of blessings, though not always an easy one. It requires surrender, trust, and a willingness to walk in alignment with God's will. But the rewards are immeasurable – a deeper relationship with God, stronger families, a greater sense of purpose, and a life overflowing with His peace and joy. It's a journey of continual growth, learning, and reliance on God's grace, a journey that leads to a life lived in the fullness of His blessings.

The gentle rustling of the leaves now seems to echo a resounding affirmation – a promise of blessings received, a testament to the power of a life lived in obedience and faithfulness to the divine plan. It is a journey well worth embarking upon, one that leads not only to personal transformation, but to the profound blessing of a family united in love, faith, and shared purpose.

## The Importance of Submissive Acts

The whispering leaves of the previous chapter's conclusion now seem to rustle with a new message, a deeper understanding of the journey we've begun. We've explored the blessings of obedience and faithfulness, but this path, this unwavering commitment to God's will, finds its truest expression in acts of submission. It's not a passive resignation, but rather an active, intentional choosing to place God and others above our own desires, mirroring the humble servanthood of Christ.

This submission, however, isn't about self-abasement or allowing ourselves to be mistreated. Instead, it's about a profound humility, a recognition of our own limitations and a willingness to place our trust in God's wisdom and guidance. It's about actively choosing to serve, to love, and to prioritize the needs of others above our own. It's a radical act of love, reflecting the very essence of Christ's sacrifice on the cross.

Consider the example of Jesus himself. He, the Son of God, humbled himself, taking on the form of a servant, and ultimately sacrificing his life for the redemption of humanity. This is the ultimate act of submission, a radical demonstration of love and obedience to the Father's will. This selfless act forms the cornerstone of our faith, reminding us that true greatness lies not in power or dominance, but in humble service. The **book of Philippians** offers a powerful illustration of this principle.

In **Philippians 2:5-8** , Paul urges us to emulate Christ's humility: "In your relationships with one another, have the same mindset as Christ Jesus: Who, being in very nature God, did not consider equality with God something to be used to his own advantage; rather, he made himself nothing by taking the very nature of a servant, being made in human likeness. And being found in appearance as a man, he humbled himself by becoming obedient to death— even death on a cross!"

This passage is not a call to passive acceptance of mistreatment, but rather a call to active, intentional humility. It's about choosing to serve, to prioritize the needs of others, and to recognize the inherent dignity of every individual. This act of submission, this relinquishing of self-importance, is transformative. It allows us to see others not as obstacles or rivals, but as fellow travelers on a shared journey of faith.

In our family relationships, submissive acts take many forms. It might be the husband choosing to prioritize his wife's needs, even when it means sacrificing his own desires. It might be the wife choosing to support her husband's dreams, even when it requires personal sacrifice. It might be a child choosing to obey his parents, even when he doesn't understand the reason behind their instructions. These are not acts of weakness, but of strength, of love, and of a deep commitment to the well-being of the family unit.

The beauty of submissive acts lies in their ripple effect. When we choose to humble ourselves, we create a space for others to do the same. We model Christ-like behavior, encouraging others to follow in our footsteps. We build trust and create a foundation for strong, healthy relationships built on mutual respect and love.

Think of the countless ways we can demonstrate submission in our daily lives. It's the act of listening attentively, even when we disagree. It's the willingness to forgive, even when it's difficult. It's the choice to extend grace, even when we feel wronged. It's the act of offering a helping hand, even when we're exhausted.

These seemingly small acts of submission accumulate, creating a powerful force for good in our homes, our communities, and the world. Furthermore, consider the context of forgiveness. Forgiveness, a cornerstone of Christian faith, is a profound act of submission. It requires us to relinquish our anger, our resentment, and our desire for retribution. It's a choice to let go of the past, to release the grip of bitterness, and to extend mercy and grace to those who have hurt us. This is a challenging act, requiring a deep well of humility and a willingness to embrace God's love and forgiveness. Forgiving others is not condoning their actions, but rather setting ourselves free from the burden of resentment.

Similarly, the act of confessing our sins is a form of submission. It requires a willingness to acknowledge our shortcomings, to lay bare our vulnerabilities, and to seek God's forgiveness. It's an act of surrender, a recognition of our dependence on God's grace and mercy. This humble confession paves the way for healing, both personally and in our relationships.

Even in our interactions with those outside our immediate family, acts of submission are essential for building strong, meaningful connections. It's the choice to serve those in need, to extend compassion to the marginalized, to speak words of encouragement to those who are discouraged. It's about seeing the image of God in every person we encounter, regardless of their background or beliefs. Consider the parable of the Good Samaritan **(Luke 10:25-37)** . The Samaritan, an unlikely hero, shows compassion to a wounded traveler, demonstrating a selfless act of submission. He sets aside his own priorities, risking his own safety to help someone in need.

This story highlights the power of selfless service, the transformative potential of a humble heart. Our commitment to submissive acts should not be driven by a desire for recognition or reward. It's not about seeking praise or approval from others. Instead, it's an expression of our love for God and our love for our fellow human beings. It's a reflection of our commitment to living a life that honors God and uplifts those around us. It is in these quiet acts of service, these seemingly small gestures of humility, that we truly find the abundant life that Christ promised.

The journey towards wholehearted faith, strong family relationships, and meaningful connections with others is a lifelong commitment. It requires constant effort, a willingness to learn and grow, and a commitment to aligning our lives with God's will. And within this journey, acts of submission play a vital, even transformative role. They are not signs of weakness, but rather powerful expressions of love, humility, and a profound connection with God and others. Through embracing these acts of submission, we not only deepen our relationship with God, but also create a space for love, forgiveness, and authentic connection to flourish in all aspects of our lives. The rustling leaves now whisper a promise of peace, a serenity that comes from a heart surrendered to God's plan, a life lived in humble service.

## A Call to Wholehearted Living

The rustling leaves of the previous chapter's conclusion have settled, their whispered promise of peace now a gentle breeze guiding us towards a deeper understanding. We've walked a path marked by obedience, faithfulness, and the transformative power of submission. We've seen how surrendering our own will to God's, mirroring the humble servitude of Christ, unlocks a wellspring of joy, peace, and authentic connection. But the journey doesn't end here; it deepens, expands, and calls us to a wholehearted embrace of faith, family, and relationships.

This is not a destination, but a continuous pilgrimage, a lifelong commitment to aligning our hearts and actions with God's divine plan. It requires courage, vulnerability, and a willingness to confront the imperfections within ourselves and the challenges we face in our relationships. It demands a constant examination of our priorities, ensuring that faith remains the unshakeable foundation upon which our families and connections are built.

Remember the parable of the mustard seed? A tiny seed, seemingly insignificant, yet capable of growing into a mighty tree, offering shelter and sustenance. Our faith, too, begins small, a seed of belief nurtured by prayer, scripture, and fellowship. But through consistent nurturing and unwavering commitment, it flourishes, transforming not only our individual lives but also the lives of those around us. Our families, our friends, our communities – all benefit from the shade and sustenance of a life lived in wholehearted devotion to God.

This wholeheartedness, this complete surrender to God's will, is not a passive resignation; it's an active participation in God's grand design. It involves conscious choices, daily decisions to prioritize God's love and guidance above our own desires. It means seeking wisdom through prayer, seeking understanding through scripture, and seeking guidance through fellowship with other believers. It's a constant conversation with God, a continuous seeking of His will in every aspect of our lives, from the mundane to the momentous. Consider the five Cs we have explored – Christ, Communication, Commitment, Compromise, and Change.

They are not merely abstract concepts, but rather the building blocks of strong, vibrant relationships rooted in faith. Christ, the cornerstone, provides the foundation of unconditional love and unwavering support. Open and honest communication builds trust and strengthens bonds, allowing for vulnerability and understanding. Commitment, the steadfast dedication to nurturing these relationships, ensures their longevity and resilience. Compromise, the willingness to set aside our own preferences for the sake of unity and harmony, fosters mutual respect and understanding. And change, the acceptance of growth and evolution within our relationships, ensures they remain dynamic and ever-evolving.

Think of your family. Are you truly present, offering unconditional love and support? Are lines of communication open, fostering honesty and vulnerability? Is there a steadfast commitment to nurturing the bonds within your family unit, even amidst challenges and disagreements? Are you willing to compromise, setting aside personal preferences for the greater good of the family? Are you embracing the inevitable changes that life brings, adapting and growing together?

And what about your other relationships? Do you extend the same principles of wholehearted living to your friendships, your work colleagues, even your acquaintances? Do you treat everyone with the same kindness, respect, and compassion that you would want to receive? The answer to these questions lies in the depth of your commitment to Christ's teachings, your willingness to live a life of love, service, and unwavering faith.

This commitment requires courage. It requires facing the difficult truths about ourselves, our shortcomings, and our areas for growth.It necessitates humility, a willingness to admit our mistakes and seek forgiveness, both from God and from those we have wronged. It demands perseverance, a steadfast commitment to upholding our values and principles even when faced with adversity. And above all, it demands faith – unwavering trust in God's plan, His wisdom, and His love for each and every one of us.

The path to wholehearted living is not always easy. It is a journey fraught with challenges, obstacles, and moments of doubt. There will be times when we stumble, when we fall short of our ideals, when we question our ability to live up to God's expectations. But it is in these moments of vulnerability that we find the greatest opportunity for growth, for deepening our relationship with God, and for strengthening the bonds within our families and relationships.

Remember that God's love is unconditional, a boundless ocean of grace and mercy. He does not demand perfection; He demands authenticity, a genuine striving towards holiness, a commitment to aligning our lives with His will. He sees our hearts, our intentions, and the efforts we make to follow Him. He understands our imperfections, our struggles, and our weaknesses. His love remains steadfast, unwavering, and eternally present, a constant source of strength and guidance on our journey.

This book is a guide, a companion on this lifelong pilgrimage. It offers biblical principles, practical examples, and personal reflections to encourage and support you on your journey towards wholehearted living. But ultimately, the journey is your own. It is a personal relationship with God, a deeply personal commitment to living a life of faith, family, and meaningful connections.

As we conclude this journey together, let us commit ourselves anew to this wholehearted approach to faith, family, and relationships. Let us strive to live each day with intention, guided by God's love and grace. Let us embrace the challenges, the triumphs, and the moments of quiet reflection, always remembering that our lives are a testament to God's unwavering love and boundless grace.

<u>Let us pray:</u> *Heavenly Father, we come before you with hearts full of gratitude for the journey we have undertaken together. We thank*

*you for the blessings in our lives, for the strength you provide, and for the guidance you offer. Help us to live lives that reflect your love, your grace, and your unwavering faithfulness. Guide us on our path towards wholehearted living, helping us to nurture our faith, strengthen our families, and build meaningful connections with those around us. We ask for your continued blessings and guidance, now and always.*

## " Amen ".

## Creator - Commitment - Communication
## Compromise     Change

## Acknowledgments

First and foremost, I offer my heartfelt thanks to God, the source of all wisdom and grace, for guiding me throughout the writing of this book. This project would have been impossible without His divine inspiration and unwavering support. I am deeply grateful to my family, whose love and patience have been a constant source of strength and encouragement. Their understanding and support during the long hours of writing were invaluable. A special thank you to my spiritual brothers, whose insightful feedback and unwavering belief in my projects proved instrumental in its completion.

I also extend my sincere gratitude to Paula Holly, whose spiritual insights help me stay on task in shaping this book into its final form. It takes spiritual insight and guidance from the Creator Himself as well.

Through His keen eye for detail with insightful suggestions enhanced the clarity and impact of the message. Finally, I want to thank all those who shared their personal stories and experiences, contributing to the authenticity and relatability of the narratives within these pages. Your willingness to be vulnerable has enriched this book immeasurably and will hopefully inspire others on their journey of faith.

## *" Iron sharpens Iron "*

## Appendix

**Pictures**
Taken by Terry Meeks and Tyree Meeks
**Bible**
New International Version
New King James Version
American Standard Version

This appendix contains additional resources to aid readers in their journey of faith, family, and relationships. Included are: Recommended books offering further insights into biblical principles of family life and relationships.

1)" Merismos "- Randy Shankle
2)" The Holy Spirit-Spiritual Gifts "- Susan Rohrer
3)" The Creator and His Creations- From My Eyes "- Terry Meeks
4)" Financial Literacy For All "- John Hope Bryant

Create a list of sample prayers for families, couples, and individuals seeking guidance and strength.

Find, add, and use from other resources:

1)
2)
3)
4)

5) Create a Christ-centered family calendar incorporating activities to strengthen faith and family bonds.

6) Discussion questions that you might have with, family, friends, individuals, couples, and small groups to facilitate deeper reflection on the book's concepts.

*" If you want to be a player in the game of life, you have to become a*

*student ".*

" **SEEK**- Salvation Enquires Enternal Knowledge "

## Glossary

This glossary provides definitions of key terms used throughout the book, clarifying concepts and providing a deeper understanding of biblical principles discussed.

**Christ-centered:** A life and relationships oriented around the teachings and example of Jesus Christ.

**Communication:** Open, honest, and empathetic sharing of thoughts and feelings.

**Commitment:** A steadfast dedication and unwavering devotion to one's faith, spouse, and family.

**Compromise:** The willingness to yield and find common ground in order to maintain harmony and respect.

**Change:** Adapting and embracing life's transitions with grace, faith, and resilience.

**Submissive Acts:** Humble acts of service and selflessness towards God and others, reflecting a Christ-like spirit.

**Sovereignty:** God's ultimate authority and control over all things. **Wholehearted:** A complete and unreserved commitment to faith, family, and relationships.

## References

**Pictures**
Taken by T. Meeks and Tyree Meeks

The biblical references used throughout this book are drawn primarily from the **New International Version (NIV)** also **American Standard Version(ASV)** Specific passages are cited within the text. " The Book of Scriptures " The Holy Bible.

### Matthew 13: 1-58 ASV
**1)** On that day Jesus went out of the house, and sat by the seaside. **2)** Great multitudes gathered to him, so that he entered into a boat, and sat, and all the multitude stood on the beach. **3)** He spoke to them many things in parables, saying, "Behold, a farmer went out to sow. **4)** As he sowed, some seeds fell by the roadside, and the birds came and devoured them. etc.

### Psalms 46:10 ASV
**10)** "Be still, and know that I am God. I will be exalted among the nations. I will be exalted in the earth."

### Ephesians 4:15 ASV
**13)** until we all attain to the unity of the faith, and of the knowledge of the Son of God, to a full grown man, to the measure of the stature of the fullness of Christ; **14)** that we may no longer be children, tossed back and forth and carried about with every wind of doctrine, by the trickery of men, in craftiness, after the wiles of error; **15) but speaking truth in love, we may grow up in all things into him, who is the head, Christ; 16)** from whom all the body, being fitted and knit together through that which every joint supplies, according to the working in measure of each individual part, makes the body increase to the building up of itself in love.

### Luke 15: 1- 32 ASV

**1)** Now all the tax collectors and sinners were coming close to him to hear him. **2)** The Pharisees and the scribes murmured, saying,"This man welcomes sinners, and eats with them." **3)** He told them this parable. **4)** "Which of you men, if you had one hundred sheep, and lost one of them, wouldn't leave the ninety-nine in the wilderness, and go after the one that was lost, until he found it? *There's more!*

### John 4 : 1-54 ASV

**1)** Therefore when the Lord knew that the Pharisees had heard that Jesus was making and baptizing more disciples than John **2)** although Jesus himself didn't baptize, but his disciples, **3)** he left Judea, and departed into Galilee. **4)** He needed to pass through Samaria. **5)** So he came to a city of Samaria, called Sychar, near the parcel of ground that Jacob gave to his son, Joseph. *There's more!*

### Matthew 6:14-15 ASV

**14)** "For if you forgive men their trespasses, your heavenly Father will also forgive you. **15)** But if you don't forgive men their trespasses, neither will youFather forgive your trespasses.

### Luke 10: 1-42 ASV

**1)** Now after these things, the Lord also appointed seventy others, and sent them two by two ahead of him into every city and place, where he was about to come. **2)** Then he said to them, "The harvest is indeed plentiful, but the laborers are few. Pray therefore to the Lord of the harvest, that he may send out laborers into his harvest. **3)** Go your ways. Behold, I send you out as lambs among wolves. **4)** Carry no purse, nor wallet, nor sandals. Greet no one on the way. **5)** Into whatever house you enter, first say, 'Peace be to this house.'etc.

### Luke 10:25-37 NIV
### Luke 10:25-37 ASV

**25)** Behold, a certain lawyer stood up and tested him, saying,"Teacher, what shall I do to inherit eternal life?" **26)** He said to him, "What is written in the law? How do you read it?" **27)** He answered, "You shall love the Lord your God with all your heart, with all your soul, with all your strength, and with all your mind; and your neighbor as yourself." **28)** He said to him, "You have answered correctly. Do this, and you will live." **29)** But he, desiring to justify himself, asked Jesus, "Who is my neighbor?" **30)** Jesus answered, "A certain man was going down from Jerusalem to Jericho, and he fell among robbers, who both stripped him and beat him, and departed, leaving him half dead. **31)** By chance a certain priest was going down that way. When he saw him, he passed by on the other side. **32)** In the same way a Levite also, when he came to the place, and saw him, passed by on the other side.

**33)** But a certain Samaritan, as he traveled, came where he was. When he saw him, he was moved with compassion, **34)** came to him, and bound up his wounds, pouring on oil and wine. He set him on his own animal, and brought him to an inn, and took care of him. **35)** On the next day, when he departed, he took out two denarii, and gave them to the host, and said to him, 'Take care of him. Whatever you spend beyond that, I will repay you when I return.' **36)** Now which of these three do you think seemed to be a neighbor to him who fell among the robbers?" **37)** He said, "He who showed mercy on him."Then Jesus said to him, "Go and do likewise."

### Matthew 18:21-35 ASV

**21)** Then Peter came and said to him, "Lord, how often shall my brother sin against me, and I forgive him? Until seven times?" **22)** Jesus said to him, "I don't tell you until seven times, but, until seventy times seven. **23)** Therefore the Kingdom of Heaven is like a certain king, who wanted to reconcile accounts with his servants. **24)** When he had begun to reconcile, one was brought to him who owed him ten thousand talents. **25)** But because he couldn't pay, his lord commanded him to be sold, with his wife, his children, and all that he had, and payment to be made. **26)** The servant therefore fell down and knelt before him, saying, 'Lord, have patience with me, and I will repay you all!' **27)** The lord of that servant, being moved with compassion, released him, and forgave him the debt. etc.

### Proverbs 15:1-3 ASV
**1)** A gentle answer turns away wrath, but a harsh word stirs up anger. 2) The tongue of the wise commends knowledge, but the mouth of fools gush out folly. **3) Yahweh's eyes are everywhere, keeping watch on the evil and the good.**

### Matthew 7:12 ASV
**11)** If you then, being evil, know how to give good gifts to your children, how much more will your Father who is in heaven give good things to those who ask him! **12)** Therefore whatever you desire for men to do to you, you shall also do to them; for this is the law and the prophets.

### Ephesians 4:26-27
**25)** Therefore putting away falsehood, speak truth each one with his neighbor. For we are members of one another. **26)** "Be angry, and don't sin." Don't let the sun go down on your wrath, **27)** and don't give place to the devil.

### Colossians 3:13 ASV
**12)** Put on therefore, as God's chosen ones, holy and beloved, a heart of compassion, kindness, lowliness, humility, and perseverance; **13)** bearing with one another, and forgiving each other, if any man has a complaint against any; even as Christ forgave you, so you also do. **14)** Above all these things, walk in love, which is the bond of perfection.

### Proverbs 18:13 NIV
**13)** He who answers before he listens—that is his folly and his shame

**Proverbs 18:11-15 ASV** **11)** The rich man's wealth is his strong city, like an unscalable wall in his own imagination. **12)**

Before destruction the heart of man is proud, but before honor is humility. **13)** He who gives answer before he hears, that is folly and shame to him. **14)** A man's spirit will sustain him in sickness, but a crushed spirit, who can bear? **15)** The heart of the discerning gets knowledge. The ear of the wise seeks knowledge.

### Philippians 2:3-11
### Philippians 2:1-11

**1)** If therefore there is any exhortation in Christ, if any consolation of love, if any fellowship of the Spirit, if any tender mercies and compassion, **2)** make my joy full, by being like-minded, having the same love, being of one accord, of one mind; **3)** doing nothing through rivalry or through conceit, but in humility, each counting others better than himself; **4)** each of you not just looking to his own things, but each of you also to the things of others. **5)** Have this in your mind, which was also in Christ Jesus, **6)** who, existing in the form of God, didn't consider equality with God a thing to be grasped, **7)** but emptied himself, taking the form of a servant, being made in the likeness of men. **8)** And being found in human form, he humbled himself, becoming obedient to the point of death, yes, the death of the cross. **9)** Therefore God also highly exalted him, and gave to him the name which is above every name; **10)** that at the name of Jesus every knee should bow, of those in heaven, those on earth, and those under the earth, **11)** and that every tongue should confess that Jesus Christ is Lord, to the glory of God the Father.

### Luke 18:1-8
### Matthew 5:44
### Galatians 6:2
### Romans 8:28Proverbs 17:6 NIV

**6)** "Children's children are the crown of old men; and the glory of children are their fathers."

### Proverbs 17:4-7 ASV

**4)** An evdoer heeds wicked lips. A liar gives ear to a mischievous tongue. **5)** Whoever mocks the poor reproaches his Maker. He who is glad at calamity shall not be unpunished. **6)** Children's children are the crown of old men; the glory of children are their parents. **7)** Arrogant speech isn't fitting for a fool, much less do lying lips fit a prince.

**Psalm 55:22**

**22)** Cast your  burdens on Yahweh, and he will sustain you. He will never allow the righteous to be removed.

**Luke 10:25-37**

"The Parable of The Good Samaritan"

## Author Biography

Terry P. Meeks is a spiritual teacher and author with a passion for helping individuals discover their relationship with God through biblical interpretation and personal spiritual growth. Studying to become a better Father, and Son of God. To give back that was given, Time, Life, and Love. Now a student of Christian nonfiction writing. Writing a series of books and articles on faith, spirituality, and personal transformation. Remembering," What is given by God, must be given back to ensure the blessing continue, in all phases of our lives". Terry P. Meeks is an active member of Destiny Christian Center-Victorville and enjoys teaching Bible Philosophy wherever it's needed, leading small groups, and mentoring others in their spiritual journeys.

Terry P. Meeks is also a passionate advocate for Time, Life, Love and believes in using their platform to make a positive impact on the world. Terry P. Meeks resides in The High Desert, with spiritual family, and friends where they continue to explore the depths of faith and share their experiences with others. They are committed to sharing their insights and experiences to inspire and empower others to break free from limitations and live their fullest potential.

## " The Legacy Continue and so does The Story "

## Copyrights

ISBN:979-8-9929877-4-4
ISBN:979-8-9929877-3-7
ISBN:979-8-9929877-5-1

Publisher: TCHC-FME-Terry Meeks
Printed in United

Author: Terry P. Meeks

tmjustchil@yahoo.com

www.ingramcontent.com/pod-product-compliance
Lightning Source LLC
Chambersburg PA
CBHW051838090426
42736CB00011B/1862